# Grand Slams, Hat Tricks and Alley-oops

# Grand Slams, Hat Tricks and Alley-oops

## A Sports Fan's Book of Words

ROBERT HENDRICKSON

Prentice Hall General Reference
*New York London Toronto Sydney Tokyo Singapore*

PRENTICE HALL GENERAL REFERENCE
15 Columbus Circle
New York, New York 10023



**Library of Congress Cataloging-in-Publication Data**

Hendrickson, Robert, 1933–
Grand slams, hat tricks and alley-oops : a sports
fan's book of words / Robert Hendrickson.
p. cm.
Includes bibliographical references and index.
ISBN 0-671-79909-6
1. Sports—Terminology. 2. Sports—Slang. I. Title.
GV567.H44 1994
796'.03—dc20 93-6421

*Designed by Rhea Braunstein*

Manufactured in the United States of America

10 9 8 7 6 5 4 3 2 1

First Edition

*For my grandson, Matthew,*
*future scholar and linebacker*

# Acknowledgments

The author would like to thank the many people, too numerous to mention here, who suggested sports expressions and recounted sports stories over the years. My thanks also to my editors, Gerry Helferich and Traci Cothran, for their suggestions and encouragement, and to my wife, Marilyn, who among scores of much warmer terms of endearment, is the "best sport" I've ever known.

# Contents

# Introduction

Before we "play ball!" or "kick off," or "get the ball rolling," a few paragraphs about our basic "game plan."

*Grand Slams, Hat Tricks and Alley-oops* is concerned mainly with the fascinating stories of words and phrases in general use that have their origins in the world of sports, not with technical sports terms used exclusively in a particular sport, of which there are many excellent collections (see the bibliography). Interesting stories of some widely known technical terms are included, as are the origins of many names of specific sports and nicknames of athletes, but the primary theme of this book is the contribution the language of sports has made to the English language as a whole since the time of Chaucer.

That contribution is a great one, as is illustrated in the more than one thousand expressions treated here that came to us from well over one hundred different sports. The sports covered range alphabetically from archery to volleyball, include all the major sports such as baseball, basketball, boxing and football, but do not neglect the so-called minor ones, even to the point of including recent fads like bungee jumping. The reader will also find many references to barbaric ancient sports such as bearbaiting and cockfighting (though today's major sports can be plenty "barbaric," too, in this age of "winning is the only thing"). Neither have I ignored hunting and fishing and games such as marbles, chess, poker, faro and roulette that have contributed so many words and phrases to the language, preferring a loose (but I think reasonable) definition of the word "sport."

"Baseball fan or not," the late Stuart Flexner wrote in *Listening to America*, "when you listen to America you hear baseball." He could just as correctly have said that when you listen to English you hear rounders, baseball, cricket, rugby, football, horse racing, boxing, track and field, tennis and scores of other sports. But baseball alone suffices in this short space to illustrate the sports terms that have become part of everyday English speech. How many of us haven't at one time or another used such common expressions as "He had two strikes against him," "I couldn't get to first base with her," "I'll take a rain check on it," "I think you're way off base on that," "He went to bat for me," "Don't throw me any more curves," "He's way out in left field," "She has a lot on the ball," "I liked her right off the bat," or even "The ballgame's not over till the last man's out"? And I've hardly "touched all the bases" with this baseball list, not to mention all the words and phrases from other sports treated in these pages. Just today I noticed the basketball expression "When the Ball Gets In His Court" as the subhead for a front-page *New York Times* article on Russian President Boris Yeltsin. And the story following used the expression "The dice aren't cast yet."

To paraphrase the astute social commentator Jacques whoever wants to know the heart and mind of America Barzun, had better learn her sports. One could add here the confirmations of many other great thinkers—but enough, we should really "get on with the game." I hope you have as good a time reading this book as I've had writing it. "Monday morning quarterbacks," "kibitzers," and FBE (Federal Bureau of Etymology) investigators will undoubtedly find omissions and errors in this wide-ranging anthology of sports words and sports lore, which I believe is the first of its kind. But if it fosters a new appreciation of the contributions sports have made to the English language and stimulates readers to discover new sports words on their own—or even if it "merely" entertains readers—I'll "know in my heart" I haven't "struck out."

—Robert Hendrickson
Peconic, N.Y.

# A

**ABET.** *Abet,* to incite, instigate or encourage someone to act, often wrongfully, derives from an old command for a dog to "sic 'em" or "go get 'em," and owes its life to the "sport" of bearbaiting, which was as popular as cricket or football in fourteenth and fifteenth century England. In bearbaiting a recently trapped bear, starved to make it unnaturally vicious, was chained to a stake or put in a pit, and a pack of dogs was set loose upon it in a fight to the death—which the bear always lost after inflicting great punishment on the dogs. Spectators who urged the dogs on were said to *abet* them, *abet* being the contraction of the Old French *abeter,* "to bait, to hound on," which in turn derived from the Norse *beita,* "to cause to bite." Bearbaiting was virtually a Sunday institution in England for eight hundred years, until it was banned in 1835; Queen Elizabeth I once attended a "Bayting" at which thirteen bears were killed.

**ABOVEBOARD.** *Aboveboard* means "honest." First recorded in the late sixteenth century, the expression derives from card playing, in which cheating is much more difficult and honesty more likely if all the hands of cards are kept above the board, or table. *Under the table,* a later expression, means "dishonest," and refers to cards manipulated under the playing surface by cardsharps.

**ACCORDING TO HOYLE.** A *Short Treatise on the Game of Whist* by Englishman Edmond Hoyle, a barrister and minor legal official in Ireland, was published in 1742. This was the first book to systemize the rules of whist (the forerunner of bridge) and remained the absolute authority for the game until its rules were changed in 1864. The author extended his range with *Hoyle's Standard Games,* which has been republished hundreds of times and is available in paperback editions today. The weight of Hoyle's authority through these works led to the phrase *according to Hoyle.* This phrase not only became a proverbial synonym for the accuracy of game rules but an idiom for correctness in general ("Let's do everything according to Hoyle."). History tells us little about Edmond Hoyle, but he enjoyed his eponymous fame for many years, living until 1769, when he died at age ninety-seven or so. Hoyle is responsible for popularizing the term "score" as a record of winning points in games. "When in doubt, win the trick" is his latter book's most memorable phrase.

**ACE IN THE HOLE.** A stud poker card dealt face down and hidden from the view of the other players is called a *hole card.* An ace is the highest hole card possible, often making a winning hand for the player holding it. Thus from this poker term came the expression *an ace in the hole* for "any hidden advantage, something held hidden in reserve until it is needed to win." The term probably dates back over a century, and was first recorded in *Collier's Magazine* in 1922: "I got a millionaire for an ace in the hole." *Hole card* is a synonym. (*See* ACES; AN ACE UP ONE'S SLEEVE; WITHIN AN ACE OF.)

**ACES.** In American slang *aces* has meant "the best" since at least the beginning of this century. The expression comes to us from the game of poker, where aces have the greatest value of all the cards. The term *ace* for "an ace flier" derives from the same source, but was first recorded in England during World War I; an air ace at the time generally had to have shot down at least five enemy planes.

*Ace,* also from poker, is now an obsolete historical term for "a run" in baseball. An *ace* in tennis, badminton and handball, among other games, is a placement made on a service of the ball, while an *ace* in golf is a hole in one. The trademarked Ace bandage, used to bind athletic injuries, uses *ace* meaning "best," too.

*Ace* figures in a large number of expressions. *To ace* a test is to receive an A on it and *ace it* means "to complete anything easily and successfully." *To be aces with* is to be highly regarded ("He's aces with the fans.") and *to ace out* is to cheat or defraud ("He aced me out of my share."). *Easy aces* in auction bridge denotes aces equally divided between opponents, while *to stand ace high,* an old saying, is to be highly esteemed. (*See* ACE IN THE HOLE; ACE UP ONE'S SLEEVE; WITHIN AN ACE OF.)

**ACESTES.** (*See* ARROW OF ACESTES.)

**ACE UP ONE'S SLEEVE.** Ever since crooked gamblers in the wild and woolly West began concealing aces up their sleeves and slipping them into their hands in card games, we have had the expression *an ace up one's sleeve* for "any tricky, hidden advantage." Although the practice is not a common way to cheat at cards anymore, the phrase lives on. (*See* ACE IN THE HOLE; WITHIN AN ACE OF.)

**ACROBAT.** *Acrobat* comes from the Greek *akros,* "aloft," plus *batos,* "climbing or walking," the word referring, of course, to the stunts early acrobats performed in the air, which included tightrope walking. The most fearless of the ancient Greek acrobats were called *neurobats,* from the Greek *neuron,* "sinew." Considered great athletes, these men performed on sinewy rope that was as thin as the catgut or plastic used for fishing line today. It appeared from the ground that they were walking on air. (*See* LEOTARDS.)

**ACROSS THE BOARD.** Around 1935, racetrack combination tickets betting on a horse to win, place or show—thus giving a bettor three chances to win—began to be called *across-the-board* bets. Since then, the term has been widely used outside the racetrack to mean "comprehensive, general, all inclusive."

**AEROBICS.** Derived from the Greek words for air and life, *aer* and *bios,* aerobic was first used to describe an organism that requires air or free oxygen for survival. Its relatively new usage was first recorded around 1965, when the physical fitness boom began in the United States. In brief, aerobics is any exercise, such as running or swimming, that stimulates and strengthens the heart and lungs, thus improving the body's use of oxygen. It can also refer to a physical fitness program based on such exercises.

**AGONY.** The Greek word from which *agony* derives had many definitions. It first meant an athletic contest; later it referred to a struggle for victory in an athletic contest. Then it meant any struggle, and finally it signified mental struggle or anguish, like Christ's in Gethsemane. The idea of physical pain and suffering wasn't a recorded meaning for *agony* until about the seventeenth century, but it's hard not to think of an athletic contest when contemplating this last definition. As one writer noted, "You only have to look at a photograph of anybody running the 100-yard dash" to understand how the word came to take on its current meaning.

**AIR BALL.** Today's fans would have trouble deciphering newspaper accounts of nineteenth-century baseball games. Consider this description of a shortstop catching a pop-up or short fly ball. Wrote a reporter in the *Chicago Times* on July 26, 1867: "Williams hit an *air ball* which was *sugared* [caught] by Barnes at short stop."

**ALIBI IKE.** Someone who is always making excuses or inventing alibis is called an *Alibi Ike.* The designation was invented by Ring Lardner in his short story "Alibi Ike" (1914) as a nickname for outfielder Frank X. Farrell, who was so named by his manager because he had excuses for everything. When Farrell drops an easy fly ball, he claims his glove "wasn't broke in yet"; when questioned about last year's batting average he replies, "I had malaria most of the season"; when he hits a triple he says he "ought to had a home run, only the ball wasn't lively," or "the wind brought it back," or he "tripped on a lump o' dirt roundin' first base"; when he takes a called third strike, he claims he "lost count" or he would have swung at and hit it. The author, who had a "phonographic ear" for American dialect, created a type for all time with Alibi Ike, and the expression became American slang as soon as the story was published. In an introduction to the yarn the incomparable Lardner noted, "The author acknowledges his indebtedness to Chief Justice Taft for some of the slang employed."

**ALL-AMERICAN.** Walter Chauncey Camp, "the Father of American Football" who formulated many of the game's rules, picked the first all-American football team in 1889 along with Caspar Whitney, a publisher of *This Week's Sport Magazine.* But the idea and designation was Whitney's and he, not Camp, should be credited with introducing *all-American* to the American lexicon of sports and other endeavors.

**ALLEY-OOP.** This interjection may have been coined by American soldiers during World War I, for it sounds like the French *allez* ("you go") plus a French pronunciation of the English *up*—hence *allez oop,* "up you go." Anyway, during the 1920s *allez-oop* (often spelled *alley-oop*) was a common interjection said upon lifting something. The expression became so popular that a caveman comic strip character was named Alley Oop. Soon *alley-oop* became a basketball term for a high pass made to a player near the basket, who then leaps to catch the ball and, in midair, stuffs it in the basket. In the late 1950s, San Francisco 49er quarterback Y. A. Tittle invented a lob pass called the *alley-oop* which was thrown over the heads of defenders to tall, former basketball player R. C. Owens.

**ALL OVER THE BALLPARK.** Anyone or anything very confused and unfocused can be said to be *all over the ballpark.* The expression, dating back to the 1950s, is from baseball, where it refers to a wild pitcher who can't find the plate.

**ALL-STAR.** The idea of an All-Star Game between the American and National baseball leagues came from *Chicago Tribune* sports editor Arch Ward in 1933. Under Ward's plan, fans voted for the players they thought were the best and the winners played in the game, earning the designation *All-Star.* In most seasons since then the fans have picked the teams, but today the balloting is conducted by the national newspaper *U.S.A. Today.* Babe Ruth hit a home run in the very first All-Star Game, or the *Midsummer Dream Game* as it is sometimes called today. That premier game was played in 1933 at Chicago's Comiskey Park as a special feature of the Chicago World's Fair.

Football's *Pro Bowl* was called the *All-Star Game* until its name was changed in 1951.

**ALSO-RAN.** The joy may be in playing, not winning, but an *also-ran* is a competitor who loses a contest. In the mid-eighteenth century, newspaper racing results listed win, place and show horses before listing all the other horses that finished out of the money under the heading "Also Ran." By 1905 the term began to be applied to politicians who lost badly in elections with a large slate of candidates, and soon it signified losers in general. From a description of an out-of-the-money race horse, an *also-ran* has come to mean any failure or any unsuccessful person. (*See* WIN, PLACE AND SHOW.)

**ALYO.** The unusual term *alyo* has had some currency in several sports for "a cool hand, a player who is not easily disconcerted." *Alyo* was probably first an underworld expression with the same meaning. It apparently derives from the Italian idiom *mangiare aglio,* literally "to eat garlic," but meaning to appear calm and placid while being angry; this idiom is rooted in the Italian folk belief that garlic wards off evil.

**AMATEUR.** An *amateur* player in any sport is one who plays for pleasure or the love of the sport rather than for financial gain or professional reasons. Appropriately, the word derives ultimately from the Latin *amator,* lover. The term was first recorded in English around 1775 and was first used in reference to sports about twenty-five years later in a description of gentlemen boxing enthusiasts. In the late nineteenth century, men vied for the title of "the world's greatest amateur athlete," and one of the leading contenders was New Yorker Foxhall Keene. (*See* CHICKEN À LA KING.)

**AMERICA'S CUP.** This racing trophy, the greatest prize in yachting, was originally called the Hundred Guinea Cup when it was offered by the British Royal Yacht Squadron to the winner of an international yacht race around the Isle of Wight. The United States schooner *America* won the first race in 1875, defeating fourteen British yachts, and the cup was renamed in her honor. American yachts won the cup in every competition until 1983, when the Australians took it home to Perth, ending the longest winning streak in the history of sports.

**ANCHOR MAN.** Usually the strongest member of the team, the runner who runs the last leg in a relay race has been called the *anchor man* since the late nineteenth century.

Possibly the term has its roots in the *anchor man* at the end of a tug-of-war team, but there is no proof that this usage came first. In any case, *anchor man* came to be applied to the last swimmer in a relay race, too, and by the 1930s was being used for the strongest member of a radio broadcasting team. With the rise of women in sports and television broadcasting the term is increasingly heard as *anchor.*

**ANGLE WITH A SILVER HOOK.** An unlucky fisherman who fails to catch anything often doesn't want to go home empty-handed. When buying fish (with silver coin, in times past) to conceal his abject failure, such a fisherman is said to *angle with a silver hook.* The term probably dates back to at least the early nineteenth century.

**ANNIE OAKLEY.** Annie Oakley was the stage name of Ohio-born Phoebe Annie Oakley Mozee (1869–1926), star rifle shot with Buffalo Bill's Wild West show. Married at sixteen, Annie joined Buffalo Bill at twenty-five and amazed audiences for more than forty years with her expert marksmanship and trick shooting. Annie once broke 942 glass balls thrown into the air with only one thousand shots. Her most famous trick was to toss a playing card, usually a five of hearts, into the air and shoot holes through all its pips. The riddled card reminded circus performers of their punched meal tickets, which they began to call *Annie Oakleys,* and the name was soon transferred to free railroad and press passes, both of which were customarily punched with a hole in the center. Today any complimentary pass, punched or not, is called an *Annie Oakley.*

**APPLE.** Calling a baseball an apple dates back to the early 1920s; before that the ball had been called a "pea." A good fielder was an *apple hawk* at the time, but this term is no longer used. A ballpark in the nineteenth century was known as an *apple orchard,* an expression that is occasionally heard today. *Apple* itself comes from the Old English *appel* for the fruit, which is, of course, round like a baseball.

**ARENA.** The floors of ancient Rome's amphitheaters had to be covered with absorbent sand because so much blood was spilled in the savage gladiatorial contests held there. The Latin word for sand is *arena,* and this became the name for the structure itself. Today the word is generally used for a *boxing arena* and for any field of conflict, activity, or endeavor, as in "the political arena."

**ARROW OF ACESTES.** In Greek legend Acestes, scion of a river god, was a great archer. Acestes had such great strength that in one contest he shot an arrow so hard that it caught fire flying through the air. Since then *arrow of Acestes* has come to mean an oratorical point made with fiery brilliance.

**ATHLETE.** Athlete comes to us from the Greek *athlon,* meaning literally "the winning of an *athlon,* or prize." Entering the English language early in the sixteenth century, the word described anyone who competed in the physical activities—running, jumping, boxing, wrestling, and the like—that formed part of the public games in ancient Greece.

**ATHLETE'S FOOT.** An advertising copywriter coined this term in 1928 in describing Absorbine Jr., a remedy for the contagious disease often caught in gyms and locker rooms; ads for Absorbine Jr. popularized the euphemism. For over four hundred years before that, *athlete's foot,* caused by a fungus that thrives on damp surfaces, had been called "ringworm." *Jock itch,* the term for a condition caused by the same fungus, was coined in the 1970s.

**AUSTRALIAN CRAWL.** Pacific Island natives probably invented this fastest of all swimming strokes and the one used by all freestyle swimmers today. But it was introduced into

Europe (where the breast stroke was the favored stroke) from Australia at the turn of the century, and thus dubbed the *Australian crawl.* (*See* TRUDGEN STROKE.)

**AXEL.** In ice skating an *axel* is a graceful leap consisting of one-and-a-half turns in the air, among other qualifications. Having nothing to do with the axle of a wheel, it is named for its inventor, Norwegian figure skater Axel Paulsen (1855–1938), who perfected it in the late nineteenth century.

# B

**BABE RUTH.** George Herman Ruth wasn't the first athlete to be called Babe, but he is certainly the most famous to bear the name, which was bestowed upon him in 1914 by a Baltimore Orioles coach, who shouted "Here's Jack's new Babe!" when Ruth (signed by Baltimore owner Jack Dunn) first entered the ballpark. Over his long career, Ruth earned many other nicknames—including *Jidge, Monk, Monkey* and the *King of Swat*—but history will always remember him as *the Babe.* A variation on this is *Bambino,* the Italian for "baby," which for centuries has meant an image of the infant Jesus in swaddling clothes.

No sports records are better known than the legendary *Sultan of Swat's* 60 home runs in one season and 714 throughout his career; and his "call" of a home run in the 1929 World Series is on every list of "most memorable sports events." There seems no reason to doubt that when all his records are broken, Babe Ruth will still be more famous than those who broke them. Ruth (1895–1948), the poor boy brought up in an orphanage who became the most renowned American athlete of all time, is one of the few people ever to become a folk hero while still alive. Some of the stories about the Bambino bear repeating. For example, he began his baseball career as a catcher for St. Mary's School in Baltimore . . . He was an outstanding pitcher in the major leagues before switching to the outfield . . . He led the major leagues in strikeouts in 1923 with 93, being a strikeout king as well as home run king

. . . He once hit a home run that literally went around the world, the ball landing in a freight car that was transported to a ship . . . His World Series performance in Chicago was not his first "call" for a home run—he had called his shot on at least one other occasion . . . And one could go on for pages from memory alone. The New York Yankees star, the Homer of Home Runs, has never been equaled for talent or color. His name will remain a synonym for the ultimate in sluggers even after someone has hit 120 homers, no matter what scandal or "real truth" is revealed about him. (*See* SULTAN OF SWAT.)

**BACKBITE.** This expression was formed from the noun *back* and the verb *bite,* possibly as an obvious description of someone slandering another person in his absence, or behind his back. But an old story connects the words with the medieval "sport" of bearbaiting, where the bear was fastened to a post by a short chain, with several fierce dogs holding him at bay, face-to-face, while others attacked him from the back. There are no known quotations to support this theory, however, the oldest one recorded (1175) referring to "Cursunge [cursing], back-titunge [backbiting] and fikelunge [deceit]."

**BACKGAMMON.** *Backgammon* takes its name from the early English *gamen,* meaning "game," the *back* in the word reflecting the strategy in the game of "sending back" pieces to the board. The game, closely related to checkers, is far older than its English name. "Back game," or *backgammon,* dates back thousands of years; in fact, a handsomely crafted backgammon board was found in the five-thousand-year-old tomb of Babylonian Queen Shub-ad.

**BACKHAND.** One of our oldest technical sports terms, *backhand* for a tennis stroke can be traced to the early eighteenth century, when Sir John Van Brugh recorded it in his play *The Mistake* (1706). The English playwright used the term figuratively, but there seems no doubt that he borrowed it from the tennis court. One hopes that Van Brugh, also the architect of massive Blenheim Palace, wasn't criticized for his backhand like he was for his buildings. A contemporary mock epitaph of him went:

*Lie heavy on him, O Earth!, for he*
*Laid many heavy loads on thee!*

**BACK THE WRONG HORSE.** When we support the wrong person, party or thing, or bet on the loser in any situation, we *back the wrong horse.* The term is an Americanism taken from the racetrack, and is still widely used although it is a century or more old.

**BACK TO SQUARE ONE.** This phrase means to "start all over again" or to "go back to the beginning" of a problem or project in an attempt to solve it. An expression of frustration, it was probably suggested by players of the various board games in which a playing piece is moved off the first square after the drawing of a card or the throw of the dice.

**BAD-BALL HITTER.** A term of recent vintage, a *bad-ball hitter* describes someone who makes bad judgments or evaluations. The Americanism refers to a batter in baseball who often swings at pitches that are not strikes and usually misses. There is no similar term in cricket or tennis. It should be noted that many batters have hit so-called bad-ball pitches for home runs, including career home run record-holder Hank Aaron, who frequently did so.

**BADGER.** Badger baiting consisted of putting a badger in a barrel or hole and setting dogs on him to "worry him out"; the cruel process was repeated several times until the badger died. The ancient "sport" gave us the expression *to badger,* "to worry or tease," even though the dogs, not the badger, did the badgering.

Centuries later *badger* was applied to the *badger game* by American con men and women. Commonly, the woman member of the team in this con game pretends to fall for her victim and goes to bed with him. While they are having sex, the male partner of the team surprises them and plays the part of the outraged husband. The victim is badgered by the "husband," who finally agrees to accept money as compensation for the wrong done him. It is sometimes months before the victim realizes he is being blackmailed, and even then he often continues making payments to avoid publicity. Figuratively, the expression *badger game* is used to indicate any deception for personal or political gain.

**BADMINTON.** This racket game, really the Indian game of *poona* adapted by the British, is named for the eighth duke of Beaufort's estate, Badminton, in Gloucestershire, where it was introduced from India in 1783. The missile hit over the net in the game is called a bird or a shuttlecock.

**BALLGAME.** (*See* THAT'S THE BALLGAME.)

**BALLPARK.** (See BALLPARK FIGURE; ALL OVER THE BALLPARK.)

**BALLPARK FIGURE.** An approximation based on an educated guess or a reasonable estimate is a ballpark figure. Only about twenty-five years old, the American expression obviously comes from baseball, *ballparks* being another name for the stadiums where baseball is played. The phrase probably derives from the 1962 coinage of *in the ballpark* for "something that is within bounds, not out of reach, or negotiable"; *out of the ballpark* means just the opposite. Baseball stadiums were first called ballparks around 1900; before then they had been called ball grounds, baseball grounds, ball fields and base ball parks.

**BALTIMORE ORIOLES.** An old dictionary tells us that the state bird of Maryland is "so called from the colors of Or (orange) and Sable in the coat of arms belonging to the second Lord Baltimore." This oriole is not closely related to the orioles of Europe, as it belongs to the blackbird and meadowlark family rather than the crow. But whatever its true species, the *Baltimore oriole* definitely takes its name from the Baltimore family, the founders of Maryland, and the bright colors of the male bird do indeed correspond to the orange and black in their heraldic arms. The city of Baltimore, Maryland, honors the Baltimores as do the early-nineteenth-century ships built in the city, the *Baltimore clippers.* The same can be said of baseball's Baltimore Orioles, who were first given the name a century ago, and football's Baltimore Colts.

**BAMBINO.** (*See* BABE RUTH.)

**BANDY-LEGGED.** Strangely enough, this word for bowlegged derives from a comparison of bowlegs with the curved sticks used in the seventeenth-century Irish game of bandy, the precursor of hockey. No one is sure where the word *bandy*—that gave us the game of *bandy, bandy-sticks,* and *bandy-legged*—comes from, though earlier it was a tennis term. In games of ancient hockey, the ball was bandied from side to side and fought for, which led to metaphors like "I'm not going to bandy words with you," that is, "I'm not going to argue or wrangle over nothing at all."

**BANGS.** A bang-tailed horse is one whose tail is allowed to grow long, and then cut or "banged off" horizontally to form an even tassel-like end. Such fashioning of horses' tails was popular in the late nineteenth century and when several bang-tailed horses won major races the style attracted wide attention. Apparently, American hair stylists or women themselves named the similar women's hair style after the horse tail style, adding *bangs* to the fashion lexicon.

**BANTAMWEIGHT.** *Bantamweight* is a class division in boxing in which the maximum weight of a fighter is 118 pounds. The name *bantam* comes from the dwarf fowl called the *bantam,* which takes its name from Bantam, Java, where it was bred centuries ago. It soon gave its name to any feisty little creature.

**BARANI ROLL.** A *barani roll* is a difficult one-and-a-half-times twist in the air in gymnastics. It has been suggested that the maneuver is named for Austrian physician Robert Barani (1876–1936) who, appropriately, won the 1914 Nobel Prize for his research into the human sense of balance.

**BARNSTORMING.** The Old English *bere,* "barley," combined with *ern,* "storage," gives us the word *barn,* which was originally a place to store grain. Only in early America did the *barn* become a joint grain storage place and animal stable, American barns becoming so big that they spawned sayings like "You couldn't hit the broad side of a barn" and "as big as a barn." *Barnstorming,* first applied in 1815 to a theatrical troupe's performances in upstate New York barns, has come to mean "tours of rural areas by political candidates" as well as baseball exhibition games played across the country and overseas by major league teams or groups of major league players after the official baseball season has ended. In the last sense it has been a good source of income for players since the early years of this century.

**BARTER.** Few, if any, American sports terms derive from the names of great players, no matter how proficient. In baseball a home run is not called a "Babe Ruth," though we may (rarely) say a "Ruthian blast"; a hitting streak is not a "DiMaggio"; nor is a strikeout a "Sandy Koufax" or "Nolan Ryan." Across the Atlantic this is not the case. *Barter,* for example, is an English cricket term dating back nearly 150 years. It comes from the name of Robert Barter, warden at Winchester College from 1832 to 1861, famed for his half-volley hits. The word is unrelated to the word "barter" meaning to trade, which is of unknown origin. (*See* BOSEY; BUCKHORSE.)

**BASEBALL.** The name of America's national pastime is first recorded in 1744 as "base ball" in *The Little Pretty Pocket Book* as a synonym for the British game of *rounders,* a direct ancestor of the sport. Another early mention of the name is found in Jane Austin's *Northhanger Abbey* (1788) in which the heroine mentions that she played *base ball* as a child. Around the turn of the century, *base ball* became *baseball.*

**BASKET.** *Basket* for a score in *basketball* comes from the half-bushel peach basket first used as a goal in the game. But *basket* wasn't the most common name for a score until about 1905—before that a score was most often termed a goal. In fact, the very first score in the first basketball game—made by one William R. Chase—was called a goal. (*See* ACCORDING TO HOYLE; BASKETBALL.)

**BASKETBALL.** The game of basketball might be called box-ball today if its inventor's intentions had been realized. Canadian James Naismith (1861–1939) invented the game while working as a physical education instructor at the International YMCA Training School (later Springfield College) in Springfield, Massachusetts, in late 1891. Though Naismith gave the game no name, simply referring to it as "the game," his plan called for hanging an overhead wooden box at each end of the school's gym. Since the school's supply room had no boxes, Naismith agreed to use two half-bushel peach baskets instead. This suggested the name *basket ball* to Naismith and he used it a month later, in January 1892, in an article for the school magazine describing the game. Soon *basket ball* was contracted to *basketball* (even though the game was first played with a soccer ball). Incidentally, Naismith's peach baskets were not cut open at the end and his players had to climb up on a ladder to retrieve each ball sunk in the basket. (*See* WHEEL.)

**BAT FOUR FOR FOUR.** (*See* BATTING A THOUSAND.)

**BATTING A THOUSAND.** Doing something perfectly. No one knows when this common saying came into the general language from baseball, but it is based on the fact that .1000 is the perfect average in baseball, with a base hit every time at bat. Variations on the phrase are *batting four hundred,* a fantastic average for a baseball hitter, and *batting three hundred,* a very good average. To *bat four for four* or *three for four* also mean "to do very well," as a baseball batter would indeed be doing if he got four or three hits in four times at bat.

**BATTING AVERAGE.** By extension, *batting average* has come to mean one's degree of achievement in any activity, but the term dates back to 1865 when it was used exclusively in baseball. In that sport, it is the measure of a player's batting ability that is obtained by dividing the number of base hits made by the number of official times at bat and carrying out the result to three decimal places. (*See* BATTING A THOUSAND.)

**BATTING EYELIDS.** To bat your eyelids is to flutter them. The expression is an Americanism that goes back to the late nineteenth century but it has nothing to do with bats flapping in a cave, someone "gone batty," or even baseball bats. In this case *batting* comes from the sport of falconry in Tudor times. According to a falconry book written in 1615: "Batting, or to bat, is when a Hawke fluttereth with his wings either from the perch or the man's fist, striving, as it were, to fly away." The old word had long been used by sportsmen and some unknown American finally found a fresh use for it in the 1880s.

**BATTLE ROYAL.** Cockfighting has a lot to do with this metaphor for a free-for-all—a battle with more than one contestant—but the expression probably didn't originate with the now outlawed "sport" as is often thought. The earliest quotations using the phrase support the theory that it derives from medieval jousting tournaments, where it was used to describe two sides fighting, each commanded by a king. Later, the term became cockpit jargon before entering standard English. In cockfighting, *battle royal* better describes what we mean by a *battle royal* today. It was an elimination tournament for gamecocks in which only the best fighters survived. A number of cocks, say eight, were thrown in the pit. These eight fought until there were only four left. Then the remaining four were rested and pitted against each other until two survived. The two survivors finally fought for the championship. American author Ralph Ellison uses the term ironically in his famous short story "Battle Royal."

**BEAT AROUND THE BUSH.** It's hard not to *beat around the bush* about the origins of this expression. Hunters once hired beaters who "started" birds and other game for them by beating the bush and scaring them out into the open. The simplest explanation for the phrase *to beat around the bush,* to approach a matter very carefully or in a roundabout way, is that these beaters had to take great care when approaching the bush or they would "start" the game too soon for the hunter to get a good shot. But British etymologist Ernest Weekley and others believe that the expression, which dates back to at least the early sixteenth century, is a mixed metaphor. Weekley suggests that the old proverb "I will not beat the bush that another may have the bird" joined with "to go around the bush"—an early expression used for a hound hesitating when circling the bush—to give us *to beat around the bush.*

**BEAT TO THE PUNCH.** British boxing champion Daniel Mendoza weighed only 160 pounds but defeated many bigger fighters with his speed and agility, which enabled him to throw a punch before his opponents could. Mendoza reigned through the 1790s, when the phrase *beat to the punch* became a common one in boxing circles. It wasn't until about thirty years later, in 1823, that *beat to the punch* began to be used figuratively for "to do what someone else plans to do before he does it." Possibly the first of the "scientific" boxers, Mendoza operated a boxing school where he taught many British gentlemen how to fight. Among many innovative techniques he originated were *infighting, the jab, the hook* and *the old one-two.* (*See* INFIGHTING.)

**BEER AND SKITTLES.** Mainly a British tavern game of nine pins in which a wooden ball or disk is used to knock down the pins, *skittles* takes its name from the Scandinavian *skutill,* "shuttle." This game, similar to shuffleboard, has been played since the early seventeenth century in taverns, where *beer and skittles* became an expression for a relaxed, laid-back lifestyle in which people want no more from life, and no less, than their beer and a game of skittles. Life sometimes gives more, of course, and frequently gives less.

**BELCHER SCARF.** Jim or Jem Belcher, England's version of Gentleman Jim Corbett, carried and made popular a large pocket handkerchief, its blue background spotted with large white spots with a small dark-blue spot in the center of each. Such handkerchiefs or neckerchiefs, often more descriptively called "bird's-eye wipes," were named *Belcher scarves* after the boxer, as was the *Belcher ring,* a huge gold affair set with a large stone that was prominent even on Belcher's massive dukes. The most celebrated boxer of his time, Belcher lost an eye in 1803 and retired from the ring to own or operate a pub. He died in 1811 when only thirty years old. Belcher's name, oddly enough, means "fine gentleman" in French. He bore a remarkable resemblance to

Napoleon and was in fact billed as the Napoleon of the Ring. (*See* PUT UP YOUR DUKES.)

**BELOW THE BELT.** Boxing rules and boxing gloves were introduced to the ring by Jack Broughton, "the Father of British Fisticuffs," in the eighteenth century. Later, teachers like Gentleman John Jackson helped improve the sport—the same Jackson who taught gamey Lord Byron how to box and about whom the poet wrote: "And men unpracticed in exchanging knocks/Must go to Jackson ere they dare to box." But much was still to be desired for the art of hitting without getting hit; brutality remained the byword in the ring and bareknuckle fighting caused many deaths and injuries every year. It remained for boxing enthusiast John Sholto Douglas, the eighth marquis of Queensberry and ancestor of Old Q (that dissolute sportsman, the fourth duke of Queensberry), to put the sport on a more humane basis. In 1867, Douglas and lightweight boxer John Graham Chambers drew up a code of twelve rules to govern boxing matches that was generally accepted by 1875 and standard throughout England by 1889. The rules instituted many modern features, including the use of gloves, a limited number of three-minute rounds, the ten-second count for a knockout, and the outlawing of wrestling, gouging, and hitting below the belt line on a boxer's trunks.

The Queensberry rules became the basis for all world boxing regulations and the first world's heavyweight champion recognized under them was American James J. "Gentleman Jim" Corbett. The rule that attracted the most attention was the one prohibiting hitting below the belt, a practice that had been widely accepted despite the fact that fighters hit in the testicles suffered excruciating pain. The Queensberry rules mark the first literal use of the expression and not long after their formulation *below the belt* was being used figuratively to describe any dirty, unfair methods. John Douglas is also remembered for his insulting letter to Oscar Wilde objecting to the author's homosexual relationship with his son Lord Alfred Douglas. Wilde sued him for libel but, although he dropped the suit, the letter revealed information that led to the poet's conviction for "immoral conduct" a short time later.

**BENDIGO.** The only city ever named for a prizefighter is *Bendigo,* Australia, which has a population of some fifty thousand and is the third largest sheep and cattle market in that country. *Bendigo,* the site of a famous gold strike in 1851, honors the ring name of English pugilist William Thompson (1811–1889), as does the *bendigo* fur cap that was popular in the late nineteenth century. Coincidentally, Thompson was born the same year that Fighting Jim Belcher died. Thompson may have been one of triplets nicknamed Shadrach, Meshac and *Abednego,* or his nickname could have stemmed from his evangelic pursuits, but in any event, in 1835 he signed his first ring challenge Abed Nego of Nottingham. He used the nickname *Bendigo* for the remainder of his career until he gave up fighting to become a full-time evangelist. *Bendigo,* Australia, had some second thoughts about its eponymous name and changed it to Sandhurst in 1871, but then reverted back to the old appellation in 1891, two years after Thompson's death. (*See* BELCHER SCARF.)

**BIG DOOLIE.** An important athlete, or any important person, is sometimes called a *big doolie,* as in this *New York Times* quote from an Olympic gold medal winner: "I got a gold today, so I'm a big doolie." The expression may have its origin in the older American slang term *dooly* meaning "dynamite," its origin unknown.

**BIG LEAGUE.** A term for major league baseball (the highest level of organized ball) since the 1890s, *big league* has come to mean the highest level in any field from art to zoology;

its antonym is another baseball term: *bush league.* (*See* BUSH LEAGUE; MAJOR LEAGUE.)

**BILK.** *Bilk* comes from the card game cribbage, where this variant of *balk* means to defraud another player of points by sharp, sly tactics. The term was widely used by the mid-1800s in its current general sense of to cheat or defraud in a clever way.

**BILL DALEY.** A long lead in a horse race is called a *Bill Daley* after a nineteenth-century American jockey instructor of that name. Bill Daley persistently advised his pupils that the best way to win a horse race is to take a long lead and hold on to it.

**BILLIARDS.** *Billiards* takes its name from the French word for the cue stick used in the game, a *billard.* The name of the game is first recorded in 1591 and Shakespeare mentions it in *Antony and Cleopatra* (1606): "Let it alone, let's to billiards."

**BINGO.** According to one good story, which I've been able to corroborate nineteenth-century Christian missionaries introduced the game of *bingo* to inhabitants in an African village while they were converting people to their religion. The people there associated the Christian concept of heaven, a Christian's final reward, with a winning player's joyous shout of "*bingo*!" and made *bingo*! their word for heaven. In any case, *bingo* is a corruption of *beano,* an early name for the game, and *beano* was patterned on *keno,* another game of chance, which takes its name from the French *quine,* for "five winning numbers."

**BIRDIE.** For well over half a century, beginning in about 1849, *bird* was American slang for "a person or thing of excellence" ("He's a perfect bird of a man"). The expression came into use at about the same time as the still used *bird* for "fellow" or "guy" ("He's a strange old bird"). In the early 1920s, possibly at the Atlantic City Country Club in New Jersey, the popular expression attached itself to golf in the form of *birdie* for "one stroke under par for a hole," which is an excellent performance. Since about 1880 *bird* has also been British slang for a girl. (*See* BADMINTON.)

**BLACK BETSY.** Probably the most famous bat in baseball was Babe Ruth's black 44-ounce bat, which he called *Black Betsy* and with which he made baseball history. No one knows for whom he named the large bat, if anyone; in fact, it may have been named *Black Betsy* by its maker, A. G. Spalding & Co. Shoeless Joe Jackson of Black Sox shame used a bat named *Black Betsy* before Ruth did. (*See* SAY IT AIN'T SO, JOE.)

**BLAZER.** The jacket called the *blazer* may take its name from the "striking blue-and-white-striped jerseys" that the captain of Britain's HMS *Blazer* ordered his crew to wear in the nineteenth century. But others say the jackets were called *blazers* because they were the "brightest possible blazing scarlet." According to this theory, the jackets were first worn by the crew of the *Lady Margaret*, St. John's College Boat Club, Cambridge, during an 1889 race on the Thames.

**BLEACHERS.** When you sit in the open outfield seats of a baseball stadium on a hot day, the sun feels strong enough to bleach your shirt. That is the humorous idea behind the coining of the word *bleachers* for cheap seats in a stadium, the term first recorded in the early 1880s. The expression now applies to all the most distant outfield seats, whether they are covered or not, and their occupants are called *bleacherites*. *Bleachers* also describes cheap seats at indoor football games, basketball games and rock concerts, among other events.

**BLINDMAN'S BUFF.** This old children's game is sometimes called "blindman's bluff," which makes no sense at all.

*Blindman's buff* is actually right, the *buff* coming from the buff, or slap on the backside, other players would give the blindfolded player when he tried to grab them to make somebody else the "blindman."

**BLINDSIDE.** For centuries *blind side* has meant the obscured part of one's field of vision. In the early 1970s, the word became a verb in professional football meaning to tackle or block an opponent from the blind side. Soon the verb was taken up generally to describe an attack on anyone who is unprepared or taken by surprise.

**BLIND TOM.** Baseball fans began calling umpires *Blind Toms* at about the turn of the century and the expression is still occasionally heard for *the boys in blue.* One theory has the often affectionate term originating with Old Blind Tom, a popular black musician in the post–Civil War era. (*See* KILL THE UMP; UMPIRE.)

**BLONDIN.** *Blondin* was the stage name of one of the greatest tightrope walkers of all time, the Frenchman Jean François Gravelet (1824–1897). The Inimitable Blondin, whose name became a synonym for a star acrobat or tightrope walker, began his career at a mere five years of age. A performer of many great feats, he was the first man to cross Niagara Falls on a tightrope, on June 30, 1859. He later made the same crossing while pushing a wheelbarrow, twirling an umbrella, and with another man on his back. The tightrope he walked was 1,100 feet long, only 3 inches thick, and was suspended 160 feet above the falls. *Blondin* is still used occasionally to describe an accomplished acrobat or nimble person. (*See* ACROBAT.)

**BLOW THE WHISTLE ON.** This phrase means to inform on someone or something. The expression, of recent vintage, was inspired by the whistles blown by basketball or football officials after a foul has been committed.

**BLUE RIBBON.** There is an interesting story behind the blue ribbon given to winners of athletic events and other competitions. Britain's highest order of knighthood is the Most Noble Order of the Garter, which has a badge of dark blue velvet ribbon edged with gold that is worn beneath the left knee. Inscribed on the ribbon in gold is the motto *Hono soit qui mal y pense* ("Shame to him who thinks evil of it"). Popular legend says that these words and the name of the order result from the gallantry of King Edward III: The king was dancing with the countess of Salisbury at a royal ball and when she lost her garter, he retrieved it and slipped it on his own leg to save her embarrassment, uttering the famous words. In any case, Edward III instituted the award in about 1344 and the blue ribbon awarded with it came to symbolize the highest honor in any field of endeavor.

**BMX.** Cross-country bicycle racing is called *BMX*, as is the cross-country bicycle itself. The *BMX* stands for *b*icycle *mo*to *c*ross, *moto* coming from the French for "motorcycle" and *cross* (X) from the English "cross-country."

**BOCCIE.** An Italian game of lawn bowling played on a dirt court shorter and narrower than a bowling green, *boccie* takes its name from the Italian *boccia*, "ball." It is often played in city parks today. (*See* SPALDING.)

**BOGEY.** *Bogey*, a word for "an imaginary or real thing that causes fear or worry," may be just a dialect form of the old word *bug*, "ghost or specter." It gives us both the *bogeyman*, who scares children, and the golf term *bogey*, for one stroke over par, which arose from a popular 1890 song called "Colonel Bogey." Bogey first meant "par" in England, because Colonel Bogey's name was adopted by golfers to signify a fictitious gentleman who could play a course or hole in the lowest number of strokes that a good golfer could play it in. American golfers, satisfied with "par" to express the British meaning of *bogey*, made Colonel Bogey something of a duffer. A *double bogey* in the United States is two strokes over par for a hole.

**BOLT FROM THE BLUE.** (*See* SHOOT ONE'S BOLT.)

**BOLT UPRIGHT.** (*See* SHOOT ONE'S BOLT.)

**BONEHEAD PLAY.** The original *bonehead play* was made on September 9, 1908, by Fred Merkle, the New York Giants first baseman. It was the last of the ninth, two outs, and the Giants had Moose McCormick on third and Merkle on first. The next man up singled to center and McCormick scored the winning run, but Merkle ran into the dugout instead of touching second base. Johnny Evers of the Cubs got the ball and stepped on second, forcing out Merkle. The winning run was nullified and the game not counted in the standings. Merkle's play became all the more important later in the season when the Cubs and Giants finished tied for first place and the Cubs won the pennant in a play-off game. Though *boneheaded* had been used in the sense of "stupid" a few years earlier, it was a sportswriter's use of *bonehead play* in reference to Merkle's blunder that introduced the phrase to the language, along with the related *to pull a boner.*

**BOO.** In *Listening to America* (1982), Stuart Berg Flexner notes that "*boo* may have been used much earlier in the theater and elsewhere, but before the 1880s [in baseball] it was considered just a roaring sound and not a word." Thus, *boo* dates back to the early nineteenth century, but *to boo* did not mean "to show disapproval" until it was first used that way in connection with baseball.

**BOOKIE.** (*See* HANDBOOK.)

**BORN WITH TWO STRIKES AGAINST HIM/HER.** It is uncertain when this expression was coined, but it clearly has its roots in baseball as an analogy to a batter only one strike away from striking out and thus failing completely. The words are usually said of someone born with great disadvantages, or of someone with incredibly bad luck.

**BOSEY.** A *bosey* is a cricketing term familiar to Australians but not much used anymore in England, where it originated. The term honors the English bowler, B. J. T. Bosanquet, who popularized the technique known elsewhere as the *googly* when he toured Australia in 1903–1904. The *googly* is, according to the *Oxford English Dictionary,* "an off-break ball bowled with leg-break action." There is no popularly known technique in American baseball, basketball or football named after its player-inventor, but there are several such eponyms in England. (*See* BARTER; BUCKHORSE.)

**BOWL GAME.** The first football *bowl game* ever recorded was the 1916 *Pasadena Bowl* (a year later renamed the *Rose Bowl*). *Bowl,* however, had been a synonym for a football stadium since 1914, when the Yale University stadium was first called the *Yale Bowl.*

**BOWLING.** Pins and balls for a sport similar to bowling were found some years ago in an Egyptian tomb dating to 5200 B.C. Bowling was long banned in England, along with football and other games, because kegling diverted men from practicing sports more valuable to a country often at war, such as archery and swordsmanship. Several English monarchs did like to bowl, though; in fact, Henry VIII built his own alley at Whitehall. The Dutch brought bowling to America and Bowling Green in New York's financial district is so named because the sport was taught there.

**BOWL OVER.** Apparently this expression meaning to surprise greatly is not from bowling nor is it an Americanism. Logan

Pearsall Smith's *Words and Idioms* (1925) claims it derives from a cricket term describing the bowler throwing the ball to the batsman. First used in England, the expression crossed the Atlantic by the end of the nineteenth century. (*See* CRICKET.)

**BOXBALL.** (*See* BASKETBALL.)

**BOX SCORE.** From its original baseball use to describe a condensed statistical record of a game that includes the performances of both teams and all the players, *box score* has taken on the extended meaning of a record of results in any area, as in the box score of an elected political figure or corporate administrator. Similar summaries of baseball games were printed in newspapers as early as 1853, but the term *box score* isn't recorded until the turn of the century, being so named because these summaries were usually printed in boxed-off sections on the sports pages of a newspaper.

**BRAINS KNOCKED OUT.** To *have one's brains knocked out* is not a modern Americanism for to be badly beaten in a fight. It dates far back to the late sixteenth century and the first British bareknuckle "fistfights," as boxing matches were called at the time. Since that time there are several recorded instances of fighters being so badly beaten in the ring that their own mothers didn't recognize them after the fight, but, thankfully, no actual cases of brains being literally knocked out. (*See* BUCKHORSE.)

**BREAKS.** A *break* means a stroke of good luck, but the term was once used only on the baseball diamond. *Lucky breaks* and *bad breaks* made up *the breaks* in general. These common terms all originated in baseball, dating back to the early years of this century and probably referring to the way a batted ball breaks away from or toward a fielder. (*See* GET A BREAK.)

**BRIDGE.** *Bridge* is a card game derived from whist that first became popular in the 1880s. Its name is of obscure origin. Since it was earlier called *biritch,* some scholars believe the word derives ultimately from the Turkish *bir,* "one," plus *iic,* "three," referring to one hand of cards in the game being exposed while the other three are concealed. Bridge was possibly introduced to Europe from the Near East, but there is no record of a Turkish game with a name anything like *bir iic.*

**BRONX CHEER.** The Bronx, one of New York City's five boroughs, takes its name from Jonas Bronck, a Dane who first settled the area for the Dutch West India Company in 1641. Points of interest in the celebrated borough are the Bronx Zoo and Botanic Gardens, the Edgar Allan Poe cottage and Yankee Stadium ("the house that Ruth built"). Long associated with baseball, the razz, or raspberry, called the *Bronx cheer,* wasn't born at Yankee Stadium, home of baseball's New York Yankees, as many baseball fans believe. It may derive from the Spanish word *branca,* "a rude shout," and possibly originated at the old National Theatre in the Bronx. We only know for certain that the term was first recorded in 1929 and that many players have received Bronx cheers in Yankee Stadium.

**BUCKHORSE.** If you gave him a few shillings the nineteenth-century English fighter John Smith, who went by the ring name *Buckhorse,* would let you punch him on the side of the head as hard as you could. The well-known boxer saw his nickname become slang for "a punch or a blow;" that is, if he saw anything but stars after a while. (*See* BARTER; BOSEY.)

**BUG.** In American racing terminology, a *bug* means the weight allowance granted to a horse because the jockey riding him is an apprentice and inexperienced; the apprentice jockey himself is also called a *bug,* or *bug boy.* This term comes from the asterisk appearing on racing forms next to the weight of a horse granted such an allowance. In printing jargon an asterisk, being small, was called a *bug*, and the term was adopted by horseplayers.

**BULLDOG.** This breed of dog takes its name from the so-called sport it was bred for, not because it bears any resemblance to a bull. Bulldogs were bred centuries ago for bull-baiting "contests" held in England until they were outlawed by Parliament in 1835. A bull was chained to a stake in the center of the arena and then whipped into a frenzy when dogs were loosed upon it. The dogs had to be able to get by the bull's horns, seize its nose and hang on tenaciously. Therefore, they were bred to be strong, savage, courageous animals with a low center of gravity and an undershot jaw. These bulldogs were often killed, but the bull could *never* win, for if it killed several bulldogs more were set upon it. Because of its courage and tenacity the bulldog became a symbol of England. Over the years the savage aggressiveness has been bred out of it. (*See* PIT BULL.)

**BULLDOGGING.** "One of the men . . . reached well over the animal's back to get a slack of the loose hide next the belly, lifting strongly, and tripped. This is called 'bulldogging.' " So did an early writer describe the way rodeo contestants wrestled steers to the ground in the American West. They often, however, leaped from their horses and twisted the cow's neck, flipping it over. Neither method suggests the way bulldogs fought bulls when such cruel contests were held in England—for the bulldog seized the bull's nose in its mouth. Esse F. O'Brien's *The First Bulldogger* (1961) therefore suggests that a black rodeo cowboy named Bill Pickett is responsible for the word; Pickett would sink his teeth into a bull's nose while wrestling it to the ground, just like bulldogs did!

**BULLPEN.** Early in this century the imposing Bull Durham Tobacco signs behind outfield fences in American baseball parks pictured a big, brightly colored bull, proclaiming that any batter whose home run hit the bull would get fifty dollars and two bags of Bull Durham. Pitchers usually warmed up near these Bull Durham signs, which may be why warm-up areas for relief pitchers are called *bullpens* today, although the word could have derived from the word *bullpen* that had meant a stockade for prisoners since 1809.

**BULL'S-EYE.** There are many plausible ways to explain this term, all of them based on a bull's eye, which is about the same size as the small black spot at the dead center of a target. *Bull's-eye* targets were not used in ancient archery contests, as is commonly thought, but were introduced to England as targets in rifle and hand-gun competitions. Perhaps the *bull's-eyes* in them were simply named for their resemblance to a bull's eye. But it is possible that *bull's-eyes* take their name from a British coin called the *bull's-eye,* which was worth a crown, or five shillings. This coin was in circulation in the early 1800s, about the time *bull's-eye* targets were introduced, and it would seem more likely that the flat target centers were named after flat coins than after the round eye of a bull. As for the coin, it was so named in the late seventeenth century, possibly because the one-crown piece was often bet on the outcome of bull-baiting contests: when a person put money "on the bull's-eye" he or she was betting on the bull, just as today we are said to put a bet on a horse's nose.

**BUMP OFF.** This underworld slang for to kill or murder may have its origins in the relatively genteel world of British boating. The theory is that *bump off* derives from a rule in boat racing that disqualified any shell that was bumped into by the boat behind it. This elimination regulation was familiar to gamblers betting on the races, proponents of the theory argue, and the term passed into the lexicon of the British underworld. Neither the *Oxford English Dictionary* nor British slang authority Eric Partridge support this theory, simply citing *bump off* as an Americanism first recorded in 1910.

**BUNGAY.** For reasons unclear, the old town of Bungay in Suffolk, England, is associated with stupidity, perhaps because Bungay sounds like "bungle." In any case, the British have long called any stupid play in whist, such as when one leads with the highest scoring card, a *bungay*.

**BUNT.** The *bunt* in baseball, used mostly by a batter as a sacrifice play to advance another runner into better scoring position, is probably a corruption of the word "butt," which does sound like *bunt* when spoken nasally. Hitters "butt" at the ball with the bat when they bunt. *Bunt* dates back to at least 1872, when the first recorded use of this strategy was made by a player named Pearce on the Brooklyn Atlantics.

**BUSH LEAGUE.** Since the turn of the century, minor league baseball leagues have been known as bush leagues because the "farm teams" belonging to them are usually located in towns "out in the bush" that are smaller and more rural than those hosting major league teams. Though bush leaguers were often farmed up to the majors, the general level of play in these leagues was far inferior to that in the big leagues and *bush league* came to mean second-rate, unprofessional, amateur or inferior in any endeavor.

**BUTTERFINGERS.** Although the word *butterfingers*—used for someone who drops things or can't hold on to anything, as if his or her fingers were coated with slippery butter—has been traced back to early-seventeenth-century England, its popularity in America stems from its use as a baseball term for a fielder who drops the ball. The baseball usage is first recorded in 1888 and *butterfingers* was being generally and widely used shortly thereafter.

**BYERLY TURK.** There are three Oriental horses from whom, without exception, all modern thoroughbred racehorses descend through the male line. *Byerly Turk,* first of the founding fathers, was the charger of English Captain Byerly at the battle of the Boyne (1690). Little is known about him except that he was a Turkish stallion purchased abroad a few years before. Darley Arabian, most celebrated of the three sires, was sent from Syria to Richard Darley of Yorkshire by his son Thomas in 1704; he was a certified Arabian stallion. Godolphin Barb or Arabian, called "the mysterious Frenchman," was brought to England from France in 1730 by Edward Coke and later sold or given to the earl of Godolphin.

# C

**CADDY.** According to legend, Mary Queen of Scots was so avid a golfer that she continued playing her round when she was informed of her husband's murder one day in 1567. An old story also claims that Mary introduced the word *cadet* (from the Gascon *capdet,* "little chief") into English from French. *Cadet* first meant the youngest son of a noble, and by 1630 meant "a young no-good who had taken to the streets"—its spelling changed to *caddy.* By the mid–eighteenth century a *caddy* came to mean a young porter on the streets and finally, a century later, a young porter who carried golf clubs. Independently, the word *cadet* for the youngest son of a nobleman came to mean a student at a military academy, because the youngest sons of nobles usually became soldiers.

**CAGER.** An early term for a basketball player still heard today. The word derives from the early net-enclosed gyms the game was played in that prevented the ball from getting into the crowd and prevented zealous spectators from getting onto the floor. (*See* BASKETBALL.)

**CALL HIS/HER BLUFF.** This widely used phrase certainly originated in American poker games of the early nineteenth century, as *bluffing* was an integral part of poker, and *to call* meant to match a bet. Some etymologists trace *bluff* itself back to the Low German *bluffen,* "to frighten by menacing conduct," which became the Dutch *buffen,* "to make a trick at cards," but *bluff* is first recorded in an 1838 newspaper account of an American poker game.

**CALL THE TURN.** Someone who *calls the turn* guesses correctly how an affair or transaction will turn out. The expression doesn't derive from the words "turn out," however; it comes to us instead from the card game faro, a very popular pastime in nineteenth-century America. One who *calls the turn* in faro, that is, one who guesses correctly what the last three cards turned over will be, wins at high odds from the bank.

**CANFIELD.** Lonely people playing solitaire can at least have the company of Richard C. Canfield (1855–1941), for this American gambler invented the world's most popular game of solitaire one summer toward the end of the nineteenth century while not active at the gaming tables of the fashionable resort of Saratoga Springs, New York. Canfield based his new game, named *canfield* after himself, on the solitaire called *klondike,* which gold miners in Alaska had invented a few decades before.

**CANTER.** Originally the *canter*—the gait of a horse between a trot and a gallop—was called a *Canterbury gallop, because it was thought to be the traditional pace of pilgrims riding to the Canterbury shrine in England.*

**CARRY THE BALL.** Any person in charge is said to *carry the ball.* Since the 1920s this football term for the player running with the ball has been used figuratively by Americans.

**CASEY AT THE BAT.** This mock heroic poem by Ernest Laurence Thayer (1863–1940) was first published in the *San Francisco Examiner* on June 3, 1888, and *Casey at the Bat* has been baseball's most famous poem ever since. Its initial popularity was due as much to Shakespearian actor De Wolf Hopper, who included the thirteen-stanza poem in his repertoire, as it was to poet Thayer, a former editor of the *Harvard Lampoon.* Everyone knows that there was no joy in Mudville when the mighty Casey struck out, but few are aware that Thayer patterned his fabled slugger on a real player, Daniel Maurice Casey, who was still posing for newspaper photographers fifty years after the poem's initial publication.

*Oh! somewhere in this favored land the*
*sun is shining bright,*
*The band is playing somewhere, and*
*somewhere hearts are light;*
*And somewhere men are laughing, and*
*somewhere children shout,*
*But there is no joy in Mudville—mighty*
*Casey has struck out.*

Dan Casey, a native of Binghamton, New York, holds no records worthy of recording—not even as a strike out king. He was a pitcher and an outfielder for Detroit and Philadelphia, but his career was overshadowed by the exploits of his older brother, Dennis, an outfielder for Baltimore and New York. Casey died in 1943, when he was seventy-eight, in Washington, D.C. As for Thayer, he was paid only five dollars for his poem, which De Wolf Hopper recited over 5,000 times. There have been more than a score of variations on his poem published since he wrote it.

**CATBIRD SEAT.** The slate-colored North American thrush (*Dumetella carolinensis*) has been called the *catbird* since the early eighteenth century because "its ordinary cry of alarm . . . somewhat resembles the mew of a cat." To *be in the catbird seat* is to be sitting pretty, like a catbird high up in a tree. It is a southern Americanism dating back to the nineteenth century but popularized nationally by Brooklyn Dodger baseball announcer Red Barber, who used it frequently in game commentaries, as well as by James Thurber's short story "The Catbird Seat."

**CATCH ON THE REBOUND.** This metaphor has been used for close to a century, and it means to capture the heart of someone after he or she has been rejected by another person. It has a sports origin and could refer to a rebound in basketball, a baseball rebounding off an outfield wall; or even a rebounding hockey puck.

**CATCH UP.** (*See* HAVE ONE'S INNINGS.)

**CAUGHT FLAT-FOOTED.** Americans have only used this expression for being caught unprepared, surprised and unready since about 1910. However, it has been traced to the reign of Queen Anne in England, where it was first applied to horses left at the "line" after the start of a horse race. These were the horses that weren't dancing forward on their toes and had all four feet flat on the ground. In fact, the term *flat-footed* for "someone with little or no hollow in the sole and a low instep," was first used to describe animals afflicted with the condition, especially horses with flat hooves and soles near the ground. Later, *caught flat-footed* must have been a good description for a runner left at the mark when a footrace began; it was eventually transferred to anyone asleep at the switch or caught unaware.

**CAULIFLOWER EAR.** The white, gnarled scar tissue that forms on an ear repeatedly injured by boxing blows gives that deformed ear the look of a head of cauliflower. The term has been around for a century or so and is even used by doctors to describe the condition.

**CELLAR.** *Cellar,* for "the lowest position in league rank for a baseball team," is first recorded in a *New York Times* headline of July 9, 1922: "Red Sox Are Up Again. Leave Cellar to Athletics by Taking Final of Series, 4 to 1." Thus the Philadelphia Athletics were the first baseball team to be etymologically *in the cellar. Cellar,* meaning "an underground room or basement'' dates back to the fourteenth century and derives from the Latin *cella* for ''cell.''

**CESTUS.** A *cestus* is a leather belt covered with metal spikes and studs that was wrapped around the fists of Greek gladiators when they stood toe-to-toe in arenas and fought to the death. The greatest cestus ''boxer'' was Theagenes of Thasos, said to have maimed or killed all 1,425 of his opponents.

**CHARLEY HORSE.** Back in 1946, the *Journal of the American Medical Association* published an article entitled ''Treatment of the Charley Horse,'' rather than ''Treatment of Injury to Quadriceps Famoris.'' This would indicate that *charley horse* has been a part of formal English for at least fifty years. But did this term for ''a leg cramp'' arise from a lame horse named Charley that pulled a roller across the infield in the Chicago White Sox ballpark in the 1890s? That's the old story, and there was such a horse but the expression was first printed several years before his baseball days, in 1887, to describe a ballplayer's stiffness or lameness. Another derivation that seems likely but hasn't been proved traces *charley horse* to the constables, or *Charleys,* of seventeenth-century England. According to this theory, *Charleys,* for ''local police,'' survived in America through the nineteenth century and because aching legs were an occupational disease among *Charleys,* ballplayers suffering such maladies were compared with the coppers and said to be ''weary from riding Charley's horse.'' Still other stories have *charley horse* deriving from a lame Baltimore Orioles pitcher named Bill Esper who walked like a lame horse (around 1894) and from a racehorse named Charley who pulled up lame in the stretch after several Oriole players bet on him (during the 1800s).

**CHECKMATE.** Chess was already an ancient game when the Persians introduced it to the Arabs. The Arabs retained the

Persian word *shah* for the king, the most important piece in the game, and when the *shah* (pronounced "shag" by the Arabs) was maneuvered into a helpless position and thus ended play, they exclaimed *shah mat* "[your] king is dead." Soon after the Arabs introduced chess into Spain in the eighth century this expression became *xaque mate,* from which derived the French *eschec mate* that finally became the English *checkmate.* For many years *checkmate* was restricted to chess, but by the fourteenth century, Chaucer and other writers were using it in the figurative sense of "to thwart, defeat, or frustrate." Our word *chess* comes from a shortening of the French *eschis,* the plural of *eschec,* so the game's name really means "kings."

**CHEERLEADER.** The young men and women who lead formal cheers at sports events began to be called *cheerleaders* in the early years of this century. The first to officially bear the name seem to have been those who cheered Amos Stagg's University of Chicago Maroons, who were a football powerhouse at the time. (*See* GRAND OLD MAN OF FOOTBALL.)

**CHICKEN À LA KING.** *Chicken à la King,* diced pieces of chicken in a sherry cream sauce, is now available canned, frozen, and even found in army mess halls, which is a long way from the éclat tables where it was served in the late nineteenth century. The dish was not invented for a king, as is popularly believed, yet it's hard to pinpoint just who *chicken à la king* does honor. Some say that New Yorker Foxhall Keene, self-proclaimed "world's greatest amateur athlete," suggested the concoction to a chef at Delmonico's. Of the numerous stories surrounding the dish's creation, the most reliable seems to be that of the famous Claridge's Hotel in London. Claridge's claimed that the dish was invented by its chef to honor J. R. Keene, whose horse had won the Grand Prix in 1881. Perhaps J. R. passed along the recipe to his son, the peerless Foxhall. At any rate, the Keenes did not hold public interest long enough, and the *Keene* in *chicken à la Keene* eventually became *king.* (*See* AMATEUR.)

**CHINESE HOME RUN.** Because Chinese immigrants were forced to work for little pay at the turn of the century, their name came to mean "cheap" in American slang and formed the basis for a number of derogatory expressions. *Chinese home run* is the only one of these that still has much currency. It describes a cheap home run where the ball just makes it over the fence. No one is sure who coined the phrase. It either arose in some ballpark on the West Coast and was brought East by the cartoonist "Tad" Dorgan (who is also responsible for the terms "yes man" and "hot dog"), or it originated in a baseball park with a fence a relatively short distance from home, possibly the 239-foot right field fence in New York's old Polo Grounds.

**CHIP IN.** Poker chips are the basis of a number of English expressions. To *chip in,* or to "share expenses," derives from the practice of players putting up their ante of chips at the start of the card game and chipping in with each bet. To *cash in one's chips,* or *hand,* that is, "to die," comes from the conclusion of a poker game, when players turn in their chips to the cashier for money. *In the chips,* another way of saying affluent, refers to having a lot of poker chips, and *the chips are down,* signifying a situation of urgency, means literally that all bets are in the pot, the hand is over and the cards now have to be shown to determine the winning hand. All of these expressions date back to the nineteenth century, when poker became our national card game. The same origin applies to a *blue-chip stock*—a high-priced common stock that pays high dividends consistently over a long period—which derives from poker's highest-valued blue chips.

**CHIP ON HIS SHOULDER.** A little-known game popular in America in the early 1800s called for a player to knock a block or chip of wood from his opponent's shoulder; the player who knocked the chip the farthest won the game. One unproved theory has it that this game is responsible for the expression *a chip on his shoulder,* describing someone easily provoked and eager to fight. The angry connotation could come from the increasing anger of the players as the game progressed, but unfortunately, since little was written about the game, no quotations have turned up to irrevocably connect the expression with it.

**CHRISTY.** Also called a *christiania,* the *christy* is a quick turn in skiing, so named for the capital of Norway—Christiania (now called Oslo)—where it was invented in the early nineteenth century.

**CLARET.** Though it hasn't been heard much since the 1930s, when radio fight announcers popularized it, *claret* is one of the oldest boxing terms. Used to describe the blood drawn in a boxing match, it is named after red claret wine; the term is recorded in the description of a boxing match held in 1604.

**CLEANUP SPOT.** *Clean up* came into the language after the gold strikes in the American West toward the end of the last century. It apparently derives from the mining term *clean up,* which describes the process of separating gold from the gravel and rock that collected in the sluices or at the stamping mill. This expression apparently gave us the term *cleanup spot* for "the fourth position in a baseball team's batting order." The batter in the cleanup slot is always a long-ball hitter who is expected to empty or clean up the bases of any teammates, that is, to bring them all home with a long hit. The term *clean up* has also come to mean "to make an exceptional financial success" or "to pull in a big haul."

**CLEVELAND INDIANS.** The winning entry in a 1915 newspaper contest to rename the Cleveland baseball team was the *Indians.* (They were formerly known as the Naps, in honor of second baseman Napoleon Lajoie, who had just retired.) The team's new name honored and still honors Louis Sockalexis, a Penobscot Indian from Old Town, Maine, who had played college ball at Holy Cross and Notre Dame before signing with Cleveland in 1897 to become the first American Indian to play in the majors. After an excellent rookie year in which he batted .338 and was known for his power hitting and strong throwing arm, Sockalexis apparently succumbed to the pressures of his situation, which included loud war whoops from the fans when he came to bat. He began drinking heavily and his playing deteriorated until he was dropped from the club in 1899. Although he played only ninety-four games, he remains the only person after whom an existing major league baseball team is named. Football's Kansas City Chiefs are named after the mayor of Kansas City, who was instrumental in bringing the franchise from Dallas to Missouri and was popularly nicknamed "the Chief." Other teams bearing "Indian" related designations include football's Washington Redskins and basketball's Golden State Warriors. Baseball's Atlanta Braves bear the name of the predecessors The Boston Braves, who were named not any American Indians but for the emblem (an Indian brave) of New York City's Tammany Hall political machine—members of which had invested in the team.

**CLUTCH PLAYER.** (*See* IN THE CLUTCH.)

**COACH.** The little village of Kocs in northwestern Hungary is responsible for the word *coach* meaning a "carriage" as well as for academic and athletic *coaches.* In the fifteenth century an unknown carriage maker in Kocs devised a larger, more comfortable carriage than any known at the time. It was called a *Koczi szeter,* a "wagon of Kocs," which was shortened to *kocsi.* Copied all over Europe, in the next century it eventually became a *coche* and then a *coach* in

English. From the name of the English horse-drawn *coach* came all *stage coaches, motor coaches,* and finally *air coaches. Coach,* for an instructor, arose as college slang; a *coach* was a figurative "carriage" whose *coaching* would "carry" you through exams. The same idea was finally applied to athletic *coaches,* who were, however, known as *coachers* up until the late 1880s.

**COCKPIT.** Belgium has long been known as the *cockpit of Europe* because so many important European battles have been fought there, from the battle of Oudenarde in 1708 to Waterloo in 1815 and the many battles of World Wars I and II. *Cockpit* is, of course, an allusion to the arena where gamecocks fight, which also gave its name to the space in fighter planes where the pilot sits.

**COLISEUM.** Its colossal size had nothing to do with the name of the Roman arena called the *Colosseum,* which gives its name to sports *coliseums.* Instead the original *Colosseum* took its name from a colossal statue of Nero that stood near it, which was placed there after the dissolute emperor's palace had been destroyed, when Rome burned while he fiddled or sang.

**COME UP TO SCRATCH.** Deaths and maimings were so frequent in the lawless early days of boxing that one rule had to be established if there were to be enough boxers left alive to please the crowd. A line was scratched in the center of the ring (in the ground or on the canvas) and a fighter who couldn't "come up to scratch" when the bell sounded for a new round was considered physically unable to fight any longer. This early version of the technical knockout probably led to use of *to come up to scratch* as a figurative expression for fulfilling or meeting requirements of any nature. *Scratch,* however, was the term for a starting point or boundary in cricket, shooting matches, horse racing and cockfighting as well as boxing, so the expression could have originated in one of these sports. Many people believe it comes from cockfighting, where a cock that doesn't *come up to scratch* and fight is considered an inferior specimen.

**COWABUNGA!** *Cowabunga!* has recently come to be used as a general cry of delight, due to the popularization of it by Bart Simpson of television fame. Originating in Australian surfing sometime in the 1960s, *cowabunga!* is still shouted by surfers at the beginning of a good ride or wave.

**COXSWAIN.** Several centuries ago a *coxswainn* was the *swain* ("boy servant") in charge of the small cock, or cock-boat, that was kept aboard for the ship's captain and used to row him to and from the ship. But with the passing of time the *coxswain* became the helmsman of any boat, regardless of size, especially the helmsman of racing sculls.

**CRAPS.** Dice have been found in ancient Egyptian tombs and in the ruins of Babylon, but the game of dice as we know it today dates to the early nineteenth century and may owe its name, *craps,* to a Frenchman. Johnny Crapaud was the sobriquet of French gambler Bernard Marigny, who introduced dice to New Orleans in about 1800 (*Crapaud* being slang for any Frenchman, owing to the belief that three *crapauds,* or toads, were the ancient arms of France). High roller Marigny became associated with the game, which was named *Johnny Crapaud's game* after his nickname, then shortened to *craps.* It is said that Marigny even named the present Burgundy Street "Craps Street" in honor of his favorite pastime.

**CRESTFALLEN.** Another term from the ancient "sport" of cockfighting, *crestfallen* refers to a defeated bird that stands waiting for the death blow with crest fallen to his beak, no longer erect and proud. Shakespeare appears to have been the first writer to apply the term to humans, in *Henry VI* (1593). (*See* SHOW THE WHITE FEATHER.)

**CRICKET.** In 1622, when villagers in Boxgrove, England near the cathedral city of Chichester were fined for playing the game of cricket on a Sunday, they cried out: "It's not cricket!" Our tale claims this is the first use of the expression and, if these villagers did say it, it seems they were just trying to get out of paying a fine. I can find no proof of the story except in the source that relates it, and the earliest I can trace the expression to is 1900, though it is foreshadowed in 1867. In any case, over the years, perhaps after the villagers paid their fine, the phrase *it's not cricket* came to mean it's unfair, it's "not playing the game." *Cricket* itself is of unknown origin, possibly coming from the Old English *cric,* "a staff," for the bat used in the game. John Gunther in *Inside Europe* (1943) writes of the British national game of cricket "and the ritualistic attitude to fair play that it has proclaimed." The quintessentially British game goes back to at least the reign of Henry VIII and it is an ancestor of baseball.

**CROQUET.** *Croquet* was made famous on expansive, immaculate English estate lawns in the mid-nineteenth century, but the sport's origins go back to France. There it was first played with a crooked stick called a *croche* (similar to a hockey stick) which eventually gave its name to the English game.

**CUE.** The long, tapering pool and billiard *cue stick* or *cue* ultimately derives from the Latin *cauda* for "tail," which went through many changes in many languages before becoming *coe* and then our *cue.* (*See* BILLIARDS.)

**CUEBALL.** A bald man, usually a completely bald one, is called a *cueball* after the round white cue ball used in the game of pool. This unflattering term is an American one dating back to World War II. (*See* CUE.)

# D

**DARK HORSE.** A wonderful story is told about a swift, coal-black horse named Dusky Pete who belonged to Tennessean Sam Flyn. Sam made an easy living riding his horse from town to town and entering him in local races because Dusky Pete looked like a lame plug but he always won handily. Sam would then collect his bets and go on to his next conquest. But this story is a fable as far as scholars are concerned. *Dark horse* was first recorded in England, not America, in about 1830. Benjamin Disraeli used it in his *The Young Duke* (1831) as a racing term that indicated more than the color of the horse: "A dark horse, which had never been thought of, rushed past the grand stand in sweeping triumph." Given Disraeli's widespread popularity as a novelist and public figure, it wasn't very long before the term was introduced in American politics to describe a candidate about whom little is known or one who wins unexpectedly. The Democratic convention of 1844 produced the first political *dark horse* in James Polk, who went on to become president, and the term was widely used by 1865.

**DARTS.** *Dart* for a pointed missile or spear is first recorded in 1314, deriving from the French *dart* meaning the same. The indoor game called *darts,* in which small darts are thrown at a target, isn't recorded in England until 1901, though this game, so popular in British pubs, must be much older.

**DAVIS CUP.** While still an undergraduate at Harvard in 1900, American statesman and sportsman Dwight Filley Davis (1879–1945) donated a silver cup to be presented as a national trophy to the country winning an international championship in lawn tennis. The cup still bears his name.

**DEAD HEAT.** Any contest—from an election to a horse race—that ends in a tie is called a *dead heat.* The expression was first used in British horseracing in the 1790s. As used here, *heat* means "a single course of a race," while *dead* suggests that the horses are "dead even," or completely even. A dead heat is a rarity in this age of electronic timing.

**DEAD MAN'S HAND.** James Butler "Wild Bill" Hickok had come to Deadwood, Dakota Territory, in 1876 at age thirty-nine to make a stake for the bride he had just taken, but lawless elements, fearing his appointment as town marshall, hired gunman Jack McCall to assassinate him, paying McCall three hundred dollars and giving him all the cheap whiskey he needed for courage. Wild Bill was playing cards in the No. 10 Saloon (his back to the open door for only the second time in his days of gunfighting) when McCall sneaked in and shot him in the back of the head, the bullet passing through his brain and striking the cardplayer across the table in the arm. Hickok's last hand, which he held tight in a death grip, was aces and eights and has ever since been called the *dead man's hand.* McCall, although freed by a packed miner's court, was later convicted by a federal court, and his plea of "double jeopardy" was disregarded on the grounds that the miner's court had no jurisdiction. He was later hanged for his crime.

**DEALING FROM THE BOTTOM OF THE DECK.** This expression passed into general use from the American poker tables of the early nineteenth century. *Dealing from the bottom of the deck,* as a crooked gambler does, means to take unfair or illegal advantage of someone, while *deal me out* means "I don't want to play this hand,'' or ''I don't want to participate this time,'' or, as Sam Goldwyn reputedly said, ''Include me out.''

**DEBONAIR.** In the medieval French sport of falconry many distinct strains of hawks were developed for hunting. But long-winged ''noble'' falcons (usually females, because males were too difficult to train) were the most prized. Such birds were said to be proud and haughty and were called *de bonne air* (''of good air''). The word was used so often by sportsmen that by the seventeenth century it came to mean any cultured or well-groomed person and it passed over into English.

**DEM BUMS.** This nickname for the Brooklyn Dodgers, beloved of memory, was given to them by an irate fan seated behind home plate at a home game in Ebbets Field during the Great Depression. Particularly incensed at one error he shouted, ''Ya bum, ya, yez bums, yez!'' Reported by a baseball writer, the fan's words stuck as an endearing nickname for the team. (*See* DODGERS.)

**DERBY.** *Derby* is the American name for a version of the dome-shaped, felt hat that the English call a bowler. The man it honors also has the *English Derby* at Churchill Downs named for him. The twelfth earl of Derby, Edward Stanley, who died in 1834, came from a family that traced its origins to William the Conqueror. He had a great interest in horse racing but little in his wife—a mutual feeling—and so, devoted most of this time to the improvement of the breed. Races had long been held at Epsom Downs, but in 1780 the earl started a series of annual contests for three-year-olds. The races were named in his honor because he suggested them and because he was such a convivial host each season at The Oaks, a house near the course that had belonged to his uncle; General ''Johnny'' Burgoyne. The *Derby* became so popular that almost a century later, in

1875, the *Kentucky Derby* adopted part of its name. After the Civil War, American spectators at the "Blue Ribbon of the Turf" noticed that English sportsmen often wore odd-shaped bowler hats. A few were brought back home, where it is said that a Connecticut manufacturer made a stiff felt, narrow-brimmed version that an unknown New York store clerk sold as "hats like the English wear at the Derby." In any event, the *derby* became not only the American term for "bowler," but the most popular headwear for men up until the 1920s.

**DEUCE.** *Deuce* for "the devil" may have its origin in the hairy demon of Celtic mythology called Dus. Other suggestions are the Old German *deurse,* "a giant," the Latin expletive *Deus*!, "My god!," or the two, or *deuce,* which is an unlucky throw (snake eyes) in a dice game. Congreve first recorded the expression *the deuce take me!* in 1694. *Deuce* for the number "two" comes from the Latin *duos,* "two."

**DEVIL'S PICTURE BOOK.** This colorful, little-known term for "playing cards" was used by the Puritans, who considered it sinful to play cards or even have a deck of cards in the house. In fact, it wasn't until the mid–nineteenth century that playing cards was deemed permissible in devout New England homes. Long before this, however, sixteenth-century clergymen issued playing cards bearing scriptural passages and Cardinal Mazarin taught France's Sun King history, geography and other subjects by printing instructive text on "educational" playing cards. We take our fifty-two-card deck from the French, but there is a fifty-six-card deck (Italian), a thirty-two-card deck (German) and many others around the world. Playing cards are also called *pasteboards* because they were made of pasteboard for centuries, the paste making them opaque so that they couldn't be seen through. It was only after 1850 that designs were printed on the backs of cards, for gamblers before that date felt that plain white backs couldn't be so easily marked as decorative ones.

**DICING.** An expression from auto racing meaning "to jockey for position on the track." The term originated in England in the 1950s, and has its origins in the old melodramatic expression "dicing with death," taking great chances.

**DIMPLES.** Englishman William Taylor is credited with manufacturing the first golf ball with *dimples,* that is, a meshlike surface made up of small depressions, in 1908. The dimples enable the ball to carry further and, in case you haven't counted, there are 360 of them on a modern golf ball. (*See* PAR FOR THE COURSE; SMILEY.)

**DISCUS.** The ancient Greek word *diskos*—which derived from the Greek *dikein,* "to throw"—was a flat, round stone or metal object thrown in athletic contests. *Diskos* passed into Latin, and finally to English as *discus,* retaining the same meaning. Because of its round shape, the *discus* gave us the words *dish, disk*—as in a *floppy disk*—and even *desk,* which originally meant a round table.

**DO A BRODIE.** Intrepid amateur athlete Steve Brodie once angered fighter Jim Corbett's father by publically predicting that John L. Sullivan would knock out his son. "So you're the fellow who jumped over the Brooklyn Bridge," the elder Corbett said when the two met for the first time shortly thereafter. "No, I jumped *off* of it," Brodie corrected him. "Oh," replied Corbett, "I thought you jumped *over* it. Any damn fool could jump off it."

But Brodie's name became proverbial as the result of his famous leap, in the form of *to do* (or *pull*) *a Brodie*—to take a great chance, even to take a suicidal leap. Brodie made his famous jump from the Manhattan side of the Brooklyn Bridge on July 23, 1886, to win a two-hundred dollar barroom bet. Eluding guards on the bridge, the twenty-three-year-old daredevil climbed to the lowest chord and plummeted 135 feet into the water below, where friends were waiting in a rowboat to retrieve him. He was arrested for endangering his life and reprimanded by a judge, but that didn't stop him from leaping off a 212-foot railroad bridge in Poughkeepsie, New York, two years later to win a five hundred dollar bet.

Brodie, who later became a successful saloonkeeper, always laughed at charges that he had really pushed a dummy off the Brooklyn Bridge. His leap was not an impossible one; about thirty years ago a man leaped off New York City's George Washington Bridge from 250 feet up, hit the water at over seventy miles an hour and then swam two hundred yards to shore.

**DODGERS.** Those incomparable Brooklyn Dodgers, who became comparable after their move to Los Angeles in 1958, were called *the Dodgers* because Manhattanites contemptuously referred to all Brooklynites as "trolley dodgers" at the turn of the century. The bustling borough was famous for its numerous trolleys, especially in the Borough Hall area. Attempts were made to change the team's name to the Superbas, the Kings and the Robins, all to no avail. Some baseball team names just seem to catch on while others don't. The Boston Bees, for example, were named by a distinguished committee of baseball writers from a list of thirteen hundred names, but people stubbornly called them the Braves, a name they retained after they moved to Milwaukee. The Cincinnati Reds tried to become known as the Redlegs to avoid identification with communism, but their name remains the Reds. (*See* DEM BUMS.)

**DOG IT.** To *dog it* is to loaf on the job, to shirk one's responsibilities and evade work. This common expression goes back to about 1920 and may come from baseball, where it means to play in this lackadaisical manner. One theory suggests it originated when an infielder lifted his leg, as a dog might, as a hard-hit grounder came at him, but the reference may simply be to the expression "a lazy dog," or "lazy as a dog."

**DOMINOES.** The *domino effect* is the political theory holding that if one country in a region is taken over by a neighbor, especially a communist one, the nearby nations will fall one after another. Also called the *domino theory,* the term was coined in about 1960 and was especially applied to South Vietnam and the rest of Southeast Asia. It is based on the way a row of pieces fall in the game of *dominoes.* The game takes its name from a likening of the pieces once used in it—then black backs and ivory faces—to black domino hoods worn by priests in medieval times.

**DON'T LOOK BACK, SOMETHING MIGHT BE GAINING ON YOU.** This is sage advice from baseball great Leroy "Satchel" Paige, who would have been one of the greatest pitchers in the major leagues if the color barrier had been broken earlier. Paige's five additional rules were: "1) avoid fried meats which angry up the blood; 2) if your stomach disputes you, lie down and pacify it with cool thoughts; 3) keep your juices flowing by jangling around gently as you move; 4) go very gently on the vices, such as carrying on in society—the social ramble ain't restful and 5) avoid running at all times."

**DOUBLE-CROSS.** *Double-cross* came into use only around 1870, apparently as an English racing term describing the common practice of winning a race after promising to arrange a *cross,* to lose it. *Cross,* for "a prearranged swindle or fix," dates back to the early nineteenth century and was used by Thackeray in *Vanity Fair* to describe a fixed horse race. The adjective *double* here is meant in its sense of "duplicity," so *double-cross* really means "dishonesty about dishonesty"; in fact, the earlier expression "to put on the double double" meant the same as *double-cross.*

**DOUBLE-HEADER.** A railroad train pulled by two locomotives was called a *double-header* in the 1870s. Though there were baseball *double-headers*—two games played in succession on the same day—as early as 1882, the term doesn't seem to have been used in baseball until the end of the century. It could have derived from the railroad usage but there is no absolute proof of this.

**DOUBLE PLAY.** Baseball's *double play,* a play in which two putouts are made, is recorded as early as 1858, but it was often called a *force play* up until the 1870s. It has since become a term Americans use when referring to any two accomplishments made at the same time.

**DOWN.** A completed play has been called a *down* in football since the late nineteenth century. *Walter Camp's Book of College Sports* (1893) explains that it was so named because a tackled ball carrier cried "down" when he was stopped by the opposite side and could go no farther. When he cried this the tacklers freed him.

**DOWN AND DIRTY.** In stud poker the last cards are dealt face down, often followed by the dealer's remark "Down and dirty," which the cards are for some of the players. From this practice came the expression *down and dirty,* meaning nasty, low, vicious and deceptive: "These are down and dirty times."

**DOWN AND OUT.** Another boxing expression which, like *down for the count,* has been used since the turn of the century. Figuratively, it can mean anything from death to abject poverty, as it does in the title of George Orwell's *Down and Out in Paris and London* (1933) as well as the movie *Down and Out in Beverly Hills.* (*See* DOWN FOR THE COUNT.)

**DOWN FOR THE COUNT.** A boxer *down for the count* is knocked out and has lost the bout; the *count* in boxing is the ten seconds a fighter has to get to his feet after being knocked down. This American expression has been around in boxing almost as long as the term *count* has been used in the sport, dating back to about 1913. Figurative use of the phrase outside of boxing came soon after. (*See* DOWN AND OUT.)

**DOWN MY ALLEY.** An alley in baseball is the imaginary line between each outfield, between right field and center field and between left field and center field. The term *right down my alley* refers to any task suitable to one's talents, and may refer to a baseball player getting easy hits down the alley. It is also possible that the expression derives from the *alley* that is the center of home plate. When a pitcher throws one right down the alley, a batter considers it an easy pitch to hit.

**DOWN TO THE WIRE.** For over a century *wire* has been synonymous for the finish line in horse racing, because of the wire stretched across the track that the horses passed under at the end of a race. The *Oxford English Dictionary* records the term from McFaul's *Ike Glidden* (1902): "The conquering colt swept under the wire for a nose ahead of the trotter." But *The Dictionary of Americanisms* cites an earlier, 1887 U.S. newspaper usage, claiming it as an Americanism and defining *wire* incorrectly as an "imaginary line marking the finish" in horse racing. Noting that the term *wire* is usually used in phrases, *The Dictionary of Americanisms* goes on to date *down to the wire* as an expression first recorded in 1950 in the newspaper account of a baseball game. Widely used as slang now for "to the very last moment or the very end," it is also heard as *to go to the wire.*

**DRAW THE LINE.** When someone says "This is where I draw the line," he or she is defining a limit beyond which that person refuses to go. Several attempts have been made to trace the sources of the figurative "line" in the phrase. One says that it referred to tennis, a sport that was almost as popular as cricket in England by the eighteenth century. When tennis was introduced from France four centuries before, it is said that there were no exact dimensions for the court and that the players drew the lines that were agreed upon. Another explanation says that *line* comes from a cut made by a plow horse across a field to indicate the boundary of a farmer's land in sixteenth-century England. No examples of the figurative expression *to draw the line* have been found before 1793, but either theory could be right. The phrase may also derive from early prizefights, where a line was drawn in the ring that neither fighter could cross.

**DRAW TO AN INSIDE STRAIGHT.** An inside straight is a very difficult straight to draw for in poker. It is so difficult, in fact, that the expression *draw to an inside straight* has become American slang for building up hope for something that has little chance of happening.

**DUMBBELLS.** Dumbbell weight machines, invented around 1850, were intricate machines where the user had to pull on ropes that lifted weights. They were patterned on the movements of bell ringers, who were often noted for their exaggerated upper body development. The machines were called *dumbbells* after the Old English word *dumb,* "mute," because there were no bells to ring on them, their name meaning "mute or silent bells." No matter how dumb some bodybuilders might be (no more so than any other group of people), the *dumb* in *dumbbell* has no connection etymologically with the word *dumb* meaning stupid.

# E

**EASY ACES.** (*See* ACES.)

**EENY, MEENY, MINY, MO.** Look in the *Oxford English Dictionary, Webster's Second,* Mathews' *Dictionary of Americanisms,* Partridge's *Dictionary of Slang,* Brewer's *Dictionary of Phrase and Fable*—in any etymological reference work—and still you will not find the "counting out" expression *eena, meena, mina, mo,* or *eeny, meeny, miny, mo,* as it is perhaps more often said. Yet this is a very familiar phrase in both the United States and Britain, used at one time or another by almost all children and frequently employed by adults. It is used in children's games to determine who will be "it" among a group of players. The full rhyme, probably dating back to the nineteenth century, was originally the insensitive (at best): "Eena, meena, mina, mo,/Catch a nigger by the toe,/If he hollers, let him go,/Eena meena, mina, mo." Sometimes the fourth line is "My Mother says I should pick this here one," and, happily, the second line is much more frequently today "Catch a tiger by the toe." The rhyme is said, of course, with the counter pointing at each player in rotation with each word, the player who is last pointed at being "it." One tradition has it that counting-out rhymes are relics of formulas Druid priests used to choose human sacrifices.

**EIGHT BALL.** In a version of rotation sometimes called Kelly pool, players must sink all fifteen balls in numerical order, except for the black eight ball, which must be pocketed last. Furthermore, if a player hits the eight ball with the cue ball prematurely, he loses points. Thus anyone who makes a shot and finds the cue ball behind or very close to the eight ball is in a difficult position, for unless he makes a difficult cushion shot, he'll probably hit the eight ball when he shoots and be penalized. From this hazardous position in Kelly pool came the expression meaning to be "in an unfortunate position with little or no hope of winning," to be "up the creek or out of luck." The words appear to be black poolroom slang dating from about 1920. The later *eight ball* for a maladjusted or inefficient person derives from the phrase (such a person is always *behind the eight ball*), with some help from the armed services "section eight" discharge for mental instability in World War II.

**ENGLISH.** The word *English*—roughly, the spin on a ball in billiards or baseball—doesn't stem from any derogatory American reference to the affectedness or tricky ways of Englishmen, as has often been proposed. It was probably suggested by *body English,* the way the body gestures or "speaks" when words cannot be found to express an action. The English call *English* "side," the term used in billiards long before its use in baseball.

**ENTER THE LISTS.** This phrase means "to compete or join in the game." *Lists* in this old expression is not a listing of names, but the borders of a field in medieval times when armed horsemen fought each other for the sport of it.

**EUCHRE.** *Euchre,* to cheat or to swindle, comes from the American card game of *euchre,* which was very popular in the West in the early nineteenth century. Gamblers cheated at the game so frequently that its name became synonymous with their chicanery.

**EXTRA INNINGS.** A baseball game that goes into *extra innings,* a term first recorded in 1885, goes beyond the normal time played (nine innings). To *go into extra innings* is said of any activity that lasts longer than usual or that takes a long time, as in "We went into extra innings on that job." The British phrase *to have a good innings* means to perform something well, but comes from the game of cricket, where an *innings* (the singular would be *inning* in baseball) is the time during which a team or player is batting.

# F

**FACE-OFF.** In hockey a face-off is the dropping of the puck by the official at the start of a game or period or to resume play. The puck is dropped between the sticks of two players, who stand face-to-face ready to hit the puck. Whether this act inspired the general term for any open confrontation (as first recorded in about 1895) is unknown, but it certainly has given the term wider currency today. (*See* HOCKEY PUCK.)

**FAIRBANKS.** Movie actor Douglas Fairbanks, Jr., was said to take great pleasure in the company of royalty. Picking up on this, contract bridge players dubbed a hand chock full of kings and queens a *fairbanks.*

**FALL GUY.** Professional wrestling a century ago wasn't as colorful as it is today but it was just as phony. There were many rigged matches and the wrestlers who agreed to take a fall, or lose a match, were dubbed *fall guys.* Soon *fall guy* became synonymous for a losing wrestler and by the first years of the new century it was being used to describe any loser or dupe.

**FAN.** *Fan* is usually held to be an Americanism derived from *fanatic* and first recorded in 1889. But another theory holds that the word comes from the term *fancy* that once described the gentlemen sports enthusiasts who attended prizefights. No one has offered ironclad proof for either derivation, but the word could have been coined at the time boxing was becoming popular with the gentry in England. *Fans* were originally sports enthusiasts, but the word has long been applied to the devoted followers of thespians as well.

*Fan* also means to strike out a batter in baseball; the word was of course suggested by the fanning of the air that occurs when a batters bat misses the ball.

**FANCY FOOTWORK.** Originally a term from American boxing describing the footwork of a skillful boxer in the ring, *fancy footwork* has come to mean any clever evasion or maneuver. It probably dates back to the early 1900s, when there were a lot of fast, clever boxers around.

**FARM OUT.** Branch Rickey, then with the St. Louis Cardinals, founded baseball's first farm system in 1918, buying stock in minor league teams on which he cultivated new players for the Cardinals. These clubs became widely known as *farm teams* and the major league players sent down to them from the parent club for more seasoning (or forever) were said to be *farmed out.* (The expression had been used for the sale of a major leaguer to the minors fifteen years or so before this.) The term is now also used to mean assigning work to another person by financial agreement, or to assign the care of a child to someone else.

**FARO.** *Faro,* which is a card game now principally played in gambling houses, derives its name from an Egyptian pharaoh, but as far as we know, from no particular king except the king of spades. The game came to England from France or Italy and little more is known about it than that. The French version was named *pharaon* (''pharaoh''), but this was altered to *faro* as its popularity grew among the English. It is assumed that at a certain stage in the game's history a likeness of an Egyptian pharaoh appeared on either all the cards, or, more likely, on the king of spades.

**FAST AS LADAS.** This literary reference is rarely heard today but should be remembered, for Alexander the Great's courier Ladas was said to run so fast that he never left a footprint. Other legendary runners include Queen Camilla of the Volsci, who, according to Virgil in the *Aeneid,* could run over water without getting her feet wet; and the Greek Iphicles, who, the Greek poet Hesiod says, could run over standing corn (wheat) without bending the ears. The Greek god Hermes (Mercury to the Romans) was swifter than all of them and was represented with wings on his sandals. (*See* MARATHON.)

**FAST SHUFFLE.** A fast shuffle by a crooked cardplayer often results in a deck stacked to that player's advantage. This has happened so often in card games that the expression *a fast shuffle* has come to mean a dishonest dealing in any enterprise.

**FATHER OF AMERICAN FOOTBALL.** While serving as a member of the Intercollegiate Football Rules Committee for forty-eight years, Walter Chauncey Camp (1859–1925) was responsible for so many rules governing American football that he can truly be said to have laid the foundations for the modern game. The Yale coach was being called the *Father of American Football* by 1920, five years before his death at one of the committee meetings. (*See* GRAND OLD MAN OF FOOTBALL.)

**FATHER OF ANGLING.** English author Izaak Walton (1593–1683) earned this title with his book on the joys of fishing, *The Compleat Angler, or the Contemplative Man's Recreation* (1653). The most quoted advice in his much quoted work: "Thus use your frog . . . Put your hook through his mouth, and out at his gills . . . and in so doing use him as though you loved him."

**FATHER OF BASEBALL.** This is the name given to Henry Chadwick, a British-born author whose writings strongly influenced the game, though he held that it evolved from the British game of rounders; to Abner Doubleday, erroneously thought to have "invented" baseball (an honor even he denied); and to Alexander Cartwright, who may indeed have "invented" the modern game.

**FEATHERWEIGHT.** (*See* LIGHTWEIGHT.)

**FELL WITH A DEAD THUD.** (*See* SPALDING.)

**FIELD.** The Anglo-Saxons called any place that had been cleared of trees a *feld,* which by the fifteenth century or so became *field* and meant "open land" as opposed to woodland. *Feld* is probably related to the Old English word *felde,* "earth." *Field* was first used to describe a baseball field in the 1845 official rules of the game and for "to catch a ball" some twenty-five years later. (*See* PLAY THE FIELD.)

**FIRE-FISHING.** An unusual sport practiced by the voyageurs and others after them, *fire-fishing* consisted of building a platform of fire on the bow of a canoe, the reflection of which would reveal any fish at the bottom of the deepest water. It is also called *torch fishing. Fire-hunting* was a method of hunting employed by some Native American tribes whereby the woods were set on fire, usually in autumn, and the animals in it were killed as they tried to escape the flames. Some colonists later adopted this "sport."

**FIRST STRING/SECOND STRING.** Archers in medieval times are responsible for these common terms for first and second sports teams. An archer was only as good as the bowstring on the stout, five-foot English longbow, and in competitions a marksman always carried two—a *fyrst-string* to be used as his best and a second to be held in reserve lest the other break. This led to the popular Elizabethan saying *two strings to his bow,* meaning to carry something in reserve in case of accident, which fathered our *first string* and *second string.*

**FISH OR CUT BAIT.** *Fish or cut bait* is an American expression that comes from fishing, meaning "to decide something one way or the other and take action." The words are first recorded in the *Congressional Record* (August 5, 1876): "Now I want you gentlemen on the other side of the House to 'fish or cut bait.' "

**FIX.** *Fix,* for the dishonest prearranging of games, races or other sports events, is an Americanism first recorded in 1881 to describe the tampering with of a horse to prevent it from winning a race. It may be a shortened version of an earlier term with the same meaning, *fix up.*

**FLAKE.** *Flake* has meant "a packet of cocaine" since the 1920s, but it first appeared in its meaning of an odd, eccentric person, often a colorful, likable eccentric person, in the 1950s, probably in baseball. It possibly referred originally to "offbeat San Francisco outfielder Jackie Brandt, from whose mind, it was said, things seemed to flake off and disappear," according to Tim Considine, writing in the *New York Times Magazine* and quoted in Paul Dickson's *The Dickson Baseball Dictionary* (1989). Then again, the *flake* of eccentricity could derive from association with the narcotics sense of the word. Stuart Berg Flexner's *Listening to America* (1982) says *flake* appeared "in professional football in the early 1970s, especially when referring to John Don Looney (who couldn't, after all, be called merely a looney . . .), who attacked tackling dummies in anger and seldom heeded signs . . ." In any case, consistent sports use of the word made it common American slang.

**FOOTBALL.** The American game of *football* has been traced back to a wild and bloody game related to the Roman game of harpastum, which had been known in England since the

Roman conquest of 43 A.D. It was essentially a free-for-all in which a pack of young men (sometimes numbering in the hundreds) would try to kick, push and butt an air-filled bladder into a rival group's area often a mile or more away. First the game was called *kicking the bladder* (a leather ball made by the local shoemaker), then during the Danish invasion, *kicking the Dane's head,* though skulls probably weren't used. The game wasn't played on a field with boundaries until the twelfth century, when the name *fut balle* was first given to it. The sport was often banned but never successfully, and it eventually evolved into *rugby football,* which became the American sport of football. (*See* FOOTBALL PLAYER; RUGBY.)

**FOOTBALL PLAYER.** Though Shakespeare did not use the modern spelling, the term *football player* is first recorded in his *King Lear* (1605): "I'll not be stricken, my Lord." "Nor tripped, neither, you base futball player." (*See* FOOTBALL.)

**FORE!** This golfing term meaning "watch out" hasn't been with us for much more than a century; it was first recorded in 1878 although the game of golf is much older. Deriving from the word *before,* "in front of," it probably was coined when the harder golf ball came into use at that time.

**FOUL BALL.** A ball hit outside of the fair playing area in baseball has been called a *foul ball* since the 1860s. By the 1920s the term was being used generally for any useless, inadequate or contemptible person, and specifically for an inferior boxer, a palooka. The great American word inventor and cartoonist T. A. Dorgan is said to be the first person to use the expression in this extended sense. More recently *foul ball* has been used to mean an outsider. (*See* PALOOKA.)

**FOUR-FLUSHER.** A person who puts on an impressive front but has no substance is called a *four-flusher.* The common species takes its name from the game or art of stud poker, in which the four cards showing can indicate a flush (five cards of the same suit) or, if the fifth card is of another suit, a useless hand. The expression dates back to the nineteenth century.

**FOUR HORSEMEN.** "Outlined against a blue-gray October sky, the Four Horsemen rode again. In dramatic lore they are known as Famine, Pestilence, Destruction, and Death. These are only aliases. Their real names are Stuhldreher, Miller, Crowley and Layden."

This was the opening of sportswriter Grantland Rice's coverage of Notre Dame's 13–7 defeat of Army at New York City's Polo Grounds on October 18, 1924, that immortalized the Notre Dame backfield. Notre Dame student publicist George Strickler seems to have suggested the name to Rice after seeing Rudolph Valentino's movie *The Four Horsemen of the Apocalypse. The Seven Mules,* for Notre Dame's line, was first suggested by Notre Dame center Adam Walsh in 1924, when, piqued by all the attention given to the backfield, he told the press: "We are just the seven mules. We do all the work so that these four fellows can gallop into fame." The expression *Four Horsemen* is a shortening of the four horsemen of the apocalypse, who are mentioned in the biblical book of Revelation, the four horsemen there being Conquest, Slaughter, Famine, and Death. Just the day before Notre Dame's backfield was dubbed *The Four Horsemen,* "Granny" Rice invented the name *The Galloping Ghost* for Illinois star runningback Red Grange. (*See* RETIRING A NUMBER.)

**FOUR-LETTER MAN.** *Four-letter man* for "an excellent athlete" originated in college sports and originally meant someone who earned a letter in football, baseball, basketball and track. Since its first use in early-twentieth-century America it has also come to be slang for a stupid person, from the four letters of *dumb,* and a contemptible person, from the four letters of *shit.* Amos Alonso Stagg, football coach at the

University of Chicago, was the first to award monograms of the first letter of a school's name to athletes and these monograms were being called *letters* by 1916. (*See* GRAND OLD MAN OF FOOTBALL.)

**FREEWHEELING.** A *freewheeling* person is one who moves about freely and independently (and who might be irresponsible), or someone who isn't governed by rules and regulations. The term comes from bicycling in the old days before the coaster brake was invented, when cyclists coasted, *free-wheeling*, down the hills. The term *freewheeler* for a bicycle is first recorded in 1889. (*See* WHEEL.)

**FRISBEE.** *Frisbee* is the trademarked name for a plastic, concave disk used in catching games between two or more players who spin the disk off with a flick of the wrist. The disk and game are said to have been inspired by a similar game played by Yale students who tossed about disposable metal pie tins that came from pies made by the Frisbee Pie Company of Bridgeport, Connecticut.

**FROM OUT OF LEFT FIELD.** (*See* OUT OF LEFT FIELD.)

**FRONT RUNNER.** *Front runner* appears to be a relatively recent addition to the language, dating back only sixty years or so. It means a person leading in any competition, especially in a political race, and derives from either track and field or horse racing.

**FULL COURT PRESS.** In basketball a very aggressive, close-guarding defense all over the court is called a *full court press.* The expression, dating back fifty or so years, is now also used to mean maximum pressure applied in any situation.

**FULL NELSON.** The name for this wrestling hold didn't come into use until the nineteenth century, when it was named either for some celebrated grappler who excelled at the pressure hold, or for a town in Lancashire, England, that was once famous for its wrestling matches. In the nineteenth century, the town changed its name from Marston to Nelson after the popular Lord Nelson Inn there, which in turn honored England's great naval hero, Viscount Horatio Nelson.

**FURLONG.** In medieval times a *furlong*—from the Old English *furh,* "furrow," and *lang,* "long"—was the length of an ideal furrow in a plowed field, which was one-eighth of a Roman mile. Though the length of furrows and other land measurements changed over the centuries, a *furlang,* changed slightly to *furlong,* remained the same eighth of a mile, or 220 yards, and became a measurement used primarily in horse racing.

# G

**GALLOPING GHOST.** (*See* FOUR HORSEMEN.)

**GAMBLE AWAY THE SUN BEFORE SUNRISE.** This saying about gold and riches might be considered the first American proverb, though it isn't recorded in *Bartlett's* or any other book of quotations. The expression surely is old enough, dating back to 1533 when Pizarro conquered Cuzco, the capital of the Inca empire, and stripped the Peruvian metropolis of gold and silver. One cavalryman's spoils included a splendid golden image of the sun so beautifully crafted that it was not melted down into coins, as was the usual practice. But that same night, before the sun had set on another day, the cavalryman lost the fabulous golden image of the sun at cards or dice. His comrades coined the saying *Juega el sol antes que amanezca*: "He gambles (or plays) away the sun before sunrise," which crossed the ocean from America on Pizarro's gold-laden galleons to become a Spanish proverb.

**GAME.** A *game* person is one who displays great courage and has the spirit of a gamecock (a cock bred and trained for cockfighting). *Gamecock* is first recorded in 1677 in the saying "Young lovers, like gamecocks, are made bolder by being kept without light," but cockfighting was brought to England by the Romans centuries before this and in the twelfth century was so popular that English schoolmasters permitted students to stage cockfighting contests, as long as all the birds killed were given to the teacher. The courage of these fighting birds was much admired and it is the likely reason that courageous people were called *game* long before the expression was first recorded in 1727.

**GAME OF THE ARROW.** American artist George Catlin recorded this favorite (though little known) game of the plains Indians: "The young men . . . assemble on the prairie [and] . . . step forward in turn, shooting their arrows into the air, endeavoring to see who can get the greatest number flying in the air at one time, thrown from the same bow."

**GAME PLAN.** Since the late 1950s *game plan* has meant the specific strategy a football team plans to use in a game. The term took on broader usage in politics and business after President Richard Nixon, an avid football fan, adopted it as a favorite expression.

**GAMESMANSHIP.** British author Stephen Potter coined this word in his 1947 book *The Theory and Practice of Gamesmanship. Gamesmanship* means "the use of dubious or seemingly improper methods that are not strictly illegal" and is almost an antonym of *sportsmanship,* upon which Potter probably based it. The subtitle of Potter's book is: *The Art of Winning Games Without Actually Cheating.*

**GAME'S NOT WORTH THE CANDLE.** In days past, card games were often played by candlelight at night. No doubt some of these nocturnal games were disparaged by high-stakes gamblers as penny ante games not worth playing in, or not worth the cost of the candle to play by, and this inspired the common expression *the game's not worth the candle.*

**GARRISON FINISH.** Holding Montana back from the pack until they came into the homestretch, "Snapper" Garrison suddenly stood high in the stirrups, bending low over the horse's mane in his famous "Yankee seat" and whipped the mount toward the finish line, moving up with a rush and winning the 1882 Suburban Handicap by a nose. This race made jockey Edward H. Garrison an American turf hero. Garrison, who died in 1931 at age seventy, used his new technique many times over his long career to win many of his races in the last furlong. The *Garrison finish* became so well known that it was applied to any close horse race, and it became synonymous with all last-minute efforts—in sports, politics or any other field.

**GARRYOWEN.** In rugby, a *garryowen* is a high punt the offensive team uses to gain ground when the forwards are rushing downfield. It takes its name from the Irish rugby club Garryowen, well known for using the tactic.

**GEE-GEE.** This term for a poor or mediocre racehorse isn't an Americanism. It can be traced back to England over 150 years ago and derives from the turning command *gee* given to a workhorse pulling a wagon. A racehorse called a *gee-gee* is thus compared to a common workhorse.

**GET A BREAK.** There are several explanations for this expression meaning "to have some good luck," but no one is certain of its origins. It has been suggested that *to get a break* might come from a *break* in pool. When a player breaks the racked balls in a pool game a good number may be pocketed, putting that player in a good position to make a long, successful run.

**GET A RISE OUT OF SOMEONE.** These words first applied to fish rising to the bait. Writers on the art of angling popularized the word *rise* in this sense three hundred years ago, and the metaphor from fly-fishing became standard English. Just as the fish rises to the bait and is caught, the person who *rises* to the lure of a practical joke becomes the butt of it. From its original meaning of raising a laugh at someone's expense, the expression has been extended to include the idea of attracting attention in general, such as getting a rise out of a sales prospect.

**GET ONE'S DUCKS IN A ROW.** American bowling alleys were the first to introduce *duck pins,* short slender bowling pins unlike the rotund pins that the English used. Pin boys who set up these pins (before the advent of automatic bowling machines) had the job of getting their ducks in a row. Soon the expression *I've got my ducks in a row* was being used by anyone who had completed any arrangements.

**GET ONE'S GOAT.** High-strung racehorses often have goats as stablemates, as goats are believed to have a calming effect on the thoroughbreds. But the horses grow attached to their companions and become upset if they are removed, thus throwing off their performance on the track. It's said that nineteenth-century gamblers capitalized on this fact by stealing the goat of a horse they wanted to lose a race. This practice may have given us the phrase *to get one's goat.* It's as good an explanation as any, but isn't supported by much evidence.

**GET READY, GET ON YOUR MARK . . .** (*See* TOE THE LINE.)

**GETTING THE UPPER HAND.** It would seem on first thought that this expression derives from the way kids choose sides with a bat in sandlot baseball. Two players, usually the best two by general agreement, participate in the choosing. One puts a hand around the bat near the fat end, then the other puts a hand around the bat just above his hand. This goes on, hand over hand, until the bottom of the bat is reached and there is no room for another hand. The last hand on the bat wins the contest (although the loser does have the chance to delicately grasp with his fingertips whatever little wood is left and twist it around his head, winning if he can hold on to the bat while doing this three times).

The winner, in any case, gets to choose first for the first player on his team and the picks are made in rotation thereafter. Perhaps this sandlot choosing popularized the expression *getting the upper hand,* "getting the best of someone," but the phrase apparently was used long before the age of sandlot baseball. It probably derives from an English game of chance that has been traced back to the fifteenth century and was played in the same way as the sandlot choosing contest.

**GET TO FIRST BASE.** Getting to first base in baseball is the first step in scoring a run, and it long ago suggested the slang expression *get to first base,* to take a successful first step or to begin well at anything. As sexual slang, *to get to first base* means "to have gotten as far as kissing." *To get to third base* means "to come close to having sexual intercourse," while *to get to home plate* (or *home*) or *to hit a homerun* means "to have sex," or to "score." Often these phrases are used to express disappointment or failure, as in "I only got to first base."

**GIMMIE.** A slang pronunciation of "give it to me," *gimmie* describes a putt of less than eighteen inches or so that is so easy that it is conceded to a player in a friendly amateur game of golf. The expression is a recent one, probably only dating back fifty years or so. (*See* DIMPLES; SMILEY.)

**GIVE AND TAKE.** The expression *give and take* is first recorded (1769) in British horse racing as "a prize for a race" in which horses over the standard height must carry more weight, and under the standard height must carry less weight. By 1816 we find the phrase being used on and off the track for making allowances or concessions in compromises. (In an interesting study of the words *give* and *take,* researchers found that over a given period among an observed group, *give* was used 2,184 times, while *take* was used 7,008 times.)

**GIVE SOMEONE A COLD DECK.** When a crooked gambler substitutes a new or "cold" deck for the used "warm" pack in a card game, the new deck is often stacked to his advantage. This practice led to the century-old expression *to give someone a cold deck* or "to shamelessly swindle a person."

**GOAL.** (*See* BASKET.)

**GOD SHOULD BE ALLOWED TO JUST WATCH THE GAME.** Yogi Berra is supposed to have made this remark from behind the plate after watching Chicago White Sox batter Minnie Minoso appeal for divine intervention by drawing a cross in the dust on home plate. The story has become sports legend, but syndicated columnist William Safire recently contacted the former Yankee catcher and Yogi denied he ever said it. *Yogiisms* Yogi hasn't denied include "I've been playing eighteen years and you can observe a lot by watching" (on his managerial abilities); "He can run anytime he wants—I'm giving him the red light" (on giving a player permission to steal a base) and the much quoted "It ain't over till it's over."

**GO FOR THE LONG BALL.** This contemporary American slang means to take a big risk for a big gain. It does not come from baseball but from football, referring to long, desperate passes made in the last minutes of a game.

**GOLF.** One guess is that the name of this sport, first recorded in 1425, comes from the Dutch word *kolf* for the club used in the game. This seems to suggest that the sport had its origins in Holland, but the first records of the game are from Scotland, although early on the Scotch did import their best-quality golf balls from Dutch makers. According to another theory *golf* may have come from the Scottish *goulf,* "to strike or cuff." Games roughly similar to golf were played as far back as Roman times, but modern day golf can be traced to Scotland's St. Andrews' course, which was built in 1552 and where, two centuries later, the Thirteen Articles laying down the rules of the sport were established.

**GOLF LINKS.** All golf courses used to be built on ridges of virtually flat land along the seashore. They were called *links* from the Old English *hlinc,* for "ridge of land."

**GOLF WIDOW.** A woman whose husband frequently leaves her alone at home while he plays golf is called a *golf widow.* The practice is much older but the term doesn't seem to have been recorded until around 1915. *Football widow* and *baseball widow* are related terms heard today.

**GOOD FIELD, NO HIT.** This baseball catch phrase is sometimes applied jokingly to other things, to anyone who does one thing better than another, who is good in one field and not another. The expression dates back to 1924, when coach Miguel "Mike" Gonzales scouted Dodger player Moe Berg for the St. Louis Cardinals. Observing Berg at Brooklyn's Clearwater, Florida, training camp that spring, Gonzales wired his boss the four-word evaluation: "Good field, no hit." The Cardinals didn't offer him a contract, but the scholarly Berg, who spoke seven languages, became an American secret agent during World War II, spying on German atomic scientists.

**GOOD SPORT.** The expression *good sport,* for one who plays fair and accepts victory or defeat amicably, is something of a redundancy, for *sport* itself has meant such a person since the end of the nineteenth century, when the expression *be a sport* was popular in England.

**GOOSE EGG.** (*See* LAY AN EGG.)

**GO SOMEONE ONE BETTER.** A common American expression today, *to go someone one better* means "to beat the performance of someone else.'' It began life as a poker term (which it still is) in the early nineteenth century, meaning to raise the bet one more chip over someone who has bet before you (''I'll go you one better'').

**GO TO BAT FOR SOMEONE.** *Going to bat for someone* means to defend, support or take up the cause of that person. This common American phrase is from baseball and was first recorded in 1916 although it was probably used earlier. The British use bats for cricket, but the phrase is not common in England.

**GO TO THE MAT.** The *mat* in wrestling is the padded canvas covering the whole floor of a wrestling ring to protect the athletes from injury. The sight of wrestlers contending on it suggested the general phrase *to go to the mat,* ''to struggle mightily in a determined, unyielding way,'' as in ''The president is going to the mat with Congress over that bill.''

**GO TO THE WIRE.** (*See* DOWN TO THE WIRE.)

**GRAND OLD MAN OF FOOTBALL.** Amos Alonzo Stagg (1862–1965), ''the Grand Old Man of Football,'' began coaching the University of Chicago football team in 1892 (after two years with the Springfield YMCA), switched over to the College of the Pacific in 1934 when he was seventy-two, and coached there until he was ninety-eight. The 5'4" Stagg was a divinity school graduate and a firm believer that football encouraged clean living and built character. It is unlikely anyone will ever break his record of seventy-five years of active coaching and only Walter Camp can match his contributions to football. The coach who never retired gave football many things, including the huddle, the single and double wingback, the shift, the man in motion, the end around or end run, the tackling dummy and letters awarded to athletes. Stagg was eighty-one when named college coach of the year in 1943, so there really is hope for all coaches. (*See* CHEERLEADER; FATHER OF AMERICAN FOOTBALL; FOUR-LETTER MAN; HUDDLE; PIGSKIN.)

**GRAND SLAM.** In bridge a *grand slam* is the taking of all thirteen tricks in a deal and the phrase dates back to about 1895 in that sense. By 1940 it became baseball's home run hit with three men on base, the bases loaded—the sport's ultimate home run. In general use, a *grand slam* is the ultimate of anything.

**GRANDSTANDING.** (*See* PLAYING TO THE GRANDSTAND.)

**GRANTLAND RICE.** (*See* RETIRING A NUMBER.)

**GREAT WHITE HOPE.** (*See* JACK JOHNSON.)

**GRIDIRON.** *Gridiron* is a football term inspired by Walter Camp, "the Father of American Football," when his rules for the game made it necessary to mark the football field with horizontal white lines at five-yard intervals. This arrangement suggested to fans that the word *gridiron* derived from *griddle* plus *iron,* for the bars running across the field did make it resemble an iron griddle or grate. But *gridiron* does not derive from *grid* plus *iron.* It was originally the name for a metal barrel griddle and comes from the Middle English *gredire,* "griddle," which in turn developed from the Old French *gridel.* (*See* FATHER OF AMERICAN FOOTBALL.)

**GUNCH.** There are words for everything if you look hard enough. A *gunch* is an attempt to influence the roll of the ball in a pinball machine game by jostling the machine. *Gunching* and *nudging* have long been common among pinball players.

**GYMNAST.** Greek athletes were required to train in the nude to allow their bodies the maximum freedom of movement. The famous Olympic track meets were run in the nude, wrestlers competed naked and all exercises were performed without clothes. Thus the Greek word *gymnazo,* "to train naked," gives us the words *gymnast* (literally someone in the nude exercising), and *gymnasium,* a place where naked exercises are done! The ancient Greeks considered the physical training of boys and young men as essential as mental training, and one of the best gymnasiums in Athens was in Plato's Academy. An amusing sidelight on all this nudity is the mineral *gymnite,* a hydrated silicate of magnesium, so named because it is found at Bare Hills, Maryland.

**HACKLE.** A *hackle* was originally an instrument used to work flax. Then the word was applied to the raised feathers of angry cockfighting fowls, which looked like they had been rumpled with a *hackle,* this usage dating back to at least 1450. Some two centuries later (no one is really sure exactly when), the first artificial fishing lures used two bright *hackles* from a gamecock as the legs of the artificial flies to be tied to the hook. Soon after *hackle* became the name of the artificial lure itself.

**HAGGARD.** Here is a word that comes from the three-thousand-year-old sport of falconry. A *haggard* bird is one trapped as an adult and very difficult to train, unlike a bird captured when a nestling. By the fourteenth century the word came to mean a wild, intractable person. Then it took on the meaning of a terrified, anxious or exhausted expression on a human face. This finally resulted in the *haggard* we use today meaning "gaunt, drawn, wasted or exhausted."

**HANDBALL.** The name of this popular sport can be traced back to fifteenth-century England but it originated in Ireland over four centuries earlier and was known as *the game of fives* for the five fingers of the hands used in it. *Handball* became popular in America in about 1882, when it is said to have been introduced by Irish immigrant Phil Casey in Brooklyn, New York.

**HANDBOOK.** Besides its standard English meaning, a *handbook* is American slang for a place where bets are made away from the racetrack, which gives us the terms *bookie* and *bookmaker,* both first recorded in the 1880s. *Handbook* was suggested by the small concealable notebooks that bookies carry for secrecy and convenience. In England, a bookmaker is called a *turf accountant* or *commission agent.*

**HANDICAP.** A sports word first used in horse racing (1754) and then in golf (since the 1870s), *handicap* may derive from an old English game called "hand in cap," which was a drawing before a horse race. "Hand in cap" was shortened to *handicap* in speech and came to mean an attempt to predict the winner of a horse race or other contest by comparing the past performances of all the contestants.

**HANG IN THERE.** This common Americanism, meaning "to refuse to give up and to stick with it," originally hails from the world of boxing, where managers exhort exhausted fighters to hang on or clinch their opponents, even to hang on to the ropes, and finish a round or a bout. In recent years the expression has come to be used as common parting words to someone in trouble, or in fact to anyone, since everyone in this life is usually up against the ropes in one way or another. Similarly, it is a frequent answer from anyone asked how he or she is: "I'm hanging in there."

**HANG IT UP.** American slang since about the 1920s for "to quit work or retire," *hang it up* is a shortened term for the baseball expression *to hang up one's spikes* ("One more season and I'll hang up my spikes") meaning the same. A less frequent variation among men is *hang up one's jockstrap,* a phrase of more recent vintage. (*See* JOCK.)

**HARDBALL.** (*See* PLAY HARDBALL.)

**HARRIER.** *Harriers* were a small breed of hounds developed to hunt hares long before they were cross-country runners. The application of the word to human runners arose out of a game called "hounds and hares" or the "paper chase," in which one team of runners (the hares) would run through the woods leaving a trail of paper scraps that the other team (the hounds) would follow, trying to catch the hares before they reached the finish line. The name *harrier* was soon given to the "hounds" and finally it became a synonym for all cross-country runners. (*See* PAPER CHASE.)

**HARRY SMITH.** Here is a sportsman whose name means "the finger," or, anyway, "two fingers," meaning the same. Harvey Smith, a well-known British show jumper, saw his name become better known after he "was alleged to have raised two fingers" at the judge of a 1971 competition. *A Harvey Smith* came to mean "the obscene gesture" in British slang, and still does, although the gesture dates back much further than Mr. Smith, and will almost certainly last longer than this probably ephemeral eponymous word.

**HAT TRICK.** British cricket bowlers in the nineteenth century were awarded a new hat, or the proceeds of a collection made by passing a hat, when they bowled down three wickets with three successful balls. This practice is the origin of the American phrase *hat trick,* used for a jockey who has three consecutive winners, a hockey or soccer player who scores three goals in one game and, less often, a baseball player who hits for the cycle (that is, a batter who hits a single, double, triple and home run in one game).

**HAVE A FIELD DAY.** Beginning in the mid–eighteenth century the British army held *field days* featuring military exercises and display. The term soon was applied to outdoor gatherings such as picnics, and then to field days at schools devoted to outdoor sports and athletic contests in which winning was not as important as having a good time. From these last field days came the expression *to have a field day* meaning to indulge oneself freely and successfully, to go all out, as in "the papers will have a field day with this story."

**HAVE ONE'S INNINGS.** *Inning* has its roots in British cricket where *innings* (always spelled with an *s* but considered singular) means a time at bat for a batsman, because that player is "in" at bat while the opposition team is "out" on the field. It is from the cricket *innings,* not baseball's borrowing of it, that we get the expression *to have one's innings,* one's opportunity or chance or one's time at bat, as it were. Other expressions stemming from cricket include *to keep one's end up, to catch up* and *to bowl over.* (*See* BOWL OVER; CRICKET.)

**HAVE THE INSIDE TRACK.** This phrase means "to have an advantageous position in any competitive situation." The expression is from American track and field and dates back to the mid–nineteenth century. The inside track or lane on a race course is the shortest and the runner positioned in it has the least distance to run (which is why many races have staggered starts).

**HAYMAKER.** Gentleman Jim Corbett used this colorful expression for a heavy, swinging blow—usually a knockout—in his autobiography, *The Roar of the Crowd* (1925). It originated a decade or so earlier, around 1910, and was popularized by radio booking announcers. The term probably derives from the slang expression *to make hay,* "to take full advantage of one's opportunities," and *the hay,* "sleep or unconsciousness." The idea of a farm worker swinging a scythe while haymaking is also suggested.

**HAZARD.** A *hazard* has come to mean "an unavoidable danger or risk, or something causing danger, peril or risk." But the word originally meant only "a dice game," a usage it still has today. This is clearly seen in the word's ancient ancestor, the Arabic *al,* "the," and *zahr,* "die." Because the cast of the dice is uncertain or risky, the word came into Spanish as *azar,* "an unexpected accident," this becoming the French *hasard,* which became the English *hazard.*

**HEAVY HITTER.** A batter who consistently hits the ball hard, a power hitter, has been called a *heavy hitter* in baseball since at least the first recording of the term in 1887. By extension the term has come to apply to anyone powerful in any profession or undertaking, giving us *political heavy hitters, literary heavy hitters,* etc.

**HEAVYWEIGHT.** A boxer who is a *heavyweight* fights in the heaviest competitive class, which is now over 175 pounds. The term has been applied to fighters in that approximate division since about 1850, although formal weight classes in boxing weren't instituted until the Queensberry rules in 1872. In the United States the boxing use of *heavyweight,* combined with an earlier (1840s) use of *heavy* for wealthy or important, led to the expression *heavyweight* for any person, company or other entity that is very powerful, influential or important. (*See* LIGHTWEIGHT.)

**HEISMAN TROPHY.** The *Heisman Memorial Trophy* has been called the ultima Thule for undergraduate football players, being awarded annually since 1935 to the best of their breed in the country. It is named for John W. Heisman, a former Georgia Tech coach whose records include a thirty-two-game unbeaten streak and the highest score ever recorded in a game, 222 to 40. Called "Shut the Gates of Mercy" Heisman, the coach was a great mentor, although he is not noted for being a gentleman on the playing field. Notable *Heisman Trophy* winners include Tom Harmon of Michigan (halfback, 1940), Paul Hornung of Notre Dame (quarterback, 1956) and O. J. Simpson of Southern California (halfback, 1968). Jay Berwanger, a University of Chicago halfback, won the initial award in 1935.

**HERMIT'S DERBY.** This is an interesting British expression, with limited American use, for "an upset victory." Hermit was the long shot that won the English Derby at Epsom Downs in 1868, his victory all the more memorable because the marquis of Hastings lost his entire fortune betting on the favorite—to the great pleasure of Hermit's owner, Henry Chaplin, whose fiancée had eloped with Lord Hastings not long before the race. (*See* LONG SHOT.)

**HIGH FIVE.** *High-fiving* is a celebratory gesture where two participants raise their hands over their heads and slap each other's hands. The *high five* is often seen after a good play in sports, and indeed, University of Louisville basketball players Wiley Brown, Daryl Cleveland and Derek Smith claimed to have invented it in 1979 during preseason practice as an odd, attention-getting gesture of triumph. However, hand slapping is also a way of greeting, especially among African-Americans. *The New Dictionary of American Slang* (1986) says the *high five* is "Chiefly used by and adopted from athletes, who themselves adopted the style from black colleagues."

**HIP! HIP! HURRAH!** The old cheer *hip! hip! hurrah!* once commonly used at sports events, has an old story attached to it, which can be taken for the little it's worth. *Hip,* we're told, derives from the Latin words H*iersolyms est* P*erdita,* "Jerusalem is destroyed." German knights, though not a very bright bunch, were supposed to have known this and shouted *hip, hip!* when they hunted people in the persecutions of the Middle Ages. *Hurrah!,* by the same strained imagining, is said to be a corruption of the Slavonic word for "paradise" (*hu-raj*). Therefore, if you ever shout *hip! hip! hurrah!* you are supposedly shouting: "Jerusalem is destroyed and we are on the road to paradise!" There is not the slightest proof of any of this, and the phrase—which doesn't date back earlier than the late eighteenth century—almost certainly comes to us from the exclamation *hip, hip, hip!* earlier used in toasts and cheers, and *huzza,* an imitative sound expressing joy and enthusiasm.

**HIPPER-DIPPER.** A *hipper-dipper* is slang for a fixed prizefight, the term dating back to the 1940s. The unusual word is of uncertain origin, but may derive from "hipper," slang for a small swimming pool, in the sense that someone takes a "dive" in it.

**HIT A HOMERUN.** (*See* GET TO FIRST BASE.)

**HIT 'EM WHERE THEY AIN'T.** Wee Willie Keeler, inventor of baseball's hit-and-run play, with New York Giants manager John McGraw contributed this expression to the language in 1897 when asked by a reporter how such a little man could have such a high batting average. (Keeler was 5'4" and weighed 140 pounds.) "Simple," Keeler advised. "I keep my eyes clear and I *hit 'em where they ain't.*" William Henry Keeler had a lifetime average of .345 over a nineteen-year career and collected 2,962 hits; he was elected to baseball's Hall of Fame in 1939. His *hit 'em where they ain't* is sometimes used outside of baseball for doing something unexpectedly, though I can find no dictionary that records the usage.

**HIT THE JACKPOT.** (*See* JACKPOT.)

**HITTING ON ALL SIXES.** In the early days of motor racing this phrase was *hitting on all fours,* referring to the four cylinders of automobiles and meaning that all the pistons in the cylinders were hitting, or firing, perfectly. With bigger cars came the expression *hitting on all six,* and though engines got even bigger, the expression never exceeded this number. Most sources have the expression as *hitting on* *all six* today, but mostly it's heard as *hitting on all sixes* to describe any good performance.

**HOCK.** (*See* IN HOCK.)

**HOCKEY PUCK.** A *hockey puck* is a fool, a lamebrain, a blockhead, a numskull or any of a hundred similar adjectives—in short, an inert someone who can offer no resistance to the blows of life or someone who is knocked around like a puck by a stick in the game of hockey. The term seems to have been coined by insult comedian Don Rickles in the early 1970s.

**HOGAN'S BRICKYARD.** Goats don't eat tin cans—they eat the paper labels off them—but these animals do stink. For this reason, and no other, anything said to be like *Hogan's goat* (a play, a book, or whatever) is something that is very bad, that really "stinks." *Hogan* is just a common name affixed to this Americanism that dates back to the turn of the century—no real person named Hogan has anything to do with it. *Hogan's brickyard,* for a rough-hewn baseball diamond—one usually in a vacant lot—is a similar expression.

**HOLD AT BAY.** Surprisingly, scholars haven't been able to connect *hold at bay* with hunting dogs that ran down big game (like stags) and held them at bay by barking, or baying, until the hunters arrived. Perhaps the baying of big-throated hounds bred for this purpose in medieval times did reinforce the expression; but *hold at bay,* to hold at a standstill, to keep someone on the defensive, derives from the French phrase *tener a bay,* which means "to hold in a state of suspense, to hold in abeyance."

**HOLD YOUR HORSES!** Harness racing at American country fairs a century and a half ago probably inspired the expression *hold your horses.* The amateur drivers, frequently young and inexperienced, often started their charges before a race had begun, leading the starter and the spectators to shout "Hold your horses!" By the 1840s the words were being used to urge human patience in general.

**HOME.** (*See* HOME RUN.)

**HOME COURT ADVANTAGE.** An expression from basketball that has become part of the American lexicon, *home court advantage* means the psychological advantage one has in familiar surroundings, where one knows the terrain better and has a sympathetic audience.

**HOME RUN.** The term *home run* in baseball was first recorded in 1856 and, as Stuart Berg Flexner pointed out in *Listening to America,* it "couldn't have appeared much sooner because it wasn't until the late 1840s and early 50s that *home* was used in games to mean the place one tried to reach in order to win or score . . ." A home run was also called a *home* at the time, but *homer* isn't recorded until 1891. It should be noted that *home run* was a cricket term before it was used in baseball. Because it is the ultimate hit in baseball, a *home run* has come to mean a great accomplishment in any field. (*See* CHINESE HOME RUN.)

**HOODWINK.** Blindman's buff was known as the "hoodwinke game" in Elizabethan times. Players would *hoodwink* or blindfold a player who would then grope around to find the others. From the game came the expression *to hoodwink* someone, "to deceive or trick a person, to leave him groping about for his money."

**HOOK, LINE AND SINKER.** Any extremely gullible person who swallows a fantastic yarn *hook, line and sinker* is like a hungry fish who gulps down not only the fisherman's baited hook but the entire tackle. This Americanism has been traced back to the age of Davy Crockett, when tall tales hooked many a fish hungry for belief. A sixteenth-century British expression, to *swallow a gudgeon* (a small bait fish), conveyed the same idea.

**HOPSCOTCH.** The Scottish people didn't invent this ancient children's game, and the *scotch* in its name had nothing to do with them, deriving instead from the lines that players hop over in the game, these being *scotched,* or scored, in the ground. In fact, the game was once called *hop-score. Hopscotch* isn't recorded until the nineteenth century.

**HORSE OF A DIFFERENT COLOR.** This expression has several explanations, but may come from races in medieval tournaments, where knights were distinguished by the color of their horses. A favored knight might have lost a race, leading one of his supporters to say, "That's a horse of a different color" as the winner crossed the finish line. But no one is sure. The phrase is first recorded in Shakespeare's *Twelfth Night,* where the expression is used as though it was familiar to the audiences of the time.

**HORSES FOR COURSES.** A mostly British expression urging someone to stick to the thing he knows best, *horses for courses* comes from the world of horse racing, where it is widely held that some horses race better on certain courses than on others. In 1898 a British writer noted, in the first recorded use of the expression: "A familiar phrase on the turf is 'horses for courses.' "

**HORSESHOES.** A game that can be traced back to the ancient Greeks, *horseshoes* is said to have originated with soldiers taking old horseshoes they had removed from their horses and tossing them for distance. These contests evolved into the game of horseshoes played by throwing horseshoes as close as possible to a stake driven into the ground thirty to forty feet away. The name for the game, however, doesn't seem to be recorded until the beginning of the nineteenth century.

**HOT DOG.** A mainstay of sports cuisine, *hot dogs* were probably first served at a sports event in New York's Polo Grounds. According to concessionaire Harry Stevens, who first served grilled franks on a heated roll there in 1901, the franks were dubbed *hot dogs* by that prolific word inventor and sports cartoonist T. A. Dorgan after he sampled them at a Giants ballgame; but Dorgan may only have popularized the word. Dorgan, or whoever invented *hot dog*, possibly had in mind the fact that many people believed frankfurters were made from dog meat at the time, and possibly heard Stevens' vendors crying out "get your red hots!," leading the indignant Coney Island chamber of commerce to ban the use of the term *hot dog* by concessionaires there (they could be called only *Coney Islands, red hots,* and *frankfurters*). *Hot dog!* became an ejaculation of approval by 1906 and is still heard occasionally. *Hot dog* is also a term for a *grandstanding* baseball player or other crowd-pleasing athletes. (*See* GRANDSTANDING.)

**HOUND SOMEONE.** *Hound* derives from the common Teutonic *hund*, related to "hunt," and may be related to the Teutonic verb *hinpan*, "to seize," in reference to big hunting dogs that actually seized their prey. Eventually, however, the designation *hound* was reserved for hunting dogs that followed their quarry by scent. There were many breeds of these from early times, but all were noted for their tenacity as well as for their keen sense of smell. Hounds would follow a trail for hours, doubling back to find a scent if they lost it. By the late sixteenth century their grim persistence had suggested the expression *to hound someone,* meaning "to relentlessly pursue a person."

**HOUSE THAT RUTH BUILT.** A familiar name for Yankee Stadium in the Bronx, New York, *the house that Ruth built* was constructed in 1923 to hold the huge crowds that came out in large part to see baseball immortal George Herman ("Babe") Ruth. Previous to this the Yankees played in the nearby Polo Grounds, which remained the home of the National League New York Giants until it was torn down years later. (Yankee Stadium was completely reconstructed in 1976.) (*See* BABE RUTH.)

**HUDDLE.** Said to have been devised by Alonzo Stagg (*see* GRAND OLD MAN OF FOOTBALL) at the University of Chicago, the *huddle* became a standard part of football's offense in the early 1920s under coach Bob Zupkke of the University of Illinois. Although named for the players huddling around the quarterback receiving instructions before each play, within ten years *huddle* became a general term for any conference on or off the football field.

**HUNTING PINK.** The famous English *hunting pink* jacket is scarlet, not pink. Moreover, it never was pink; its name comes from the London tailor named Pink who designed it for fox hunting in the eighteenth century.

**HUSH PUPPY.** These cakes of deep-fried cornmeal batter, which are very popular in the South, have been traced back only to the time of World War I; at least the name isn't recorded before then. The most common explanation for the odd name is that hunters tossed bits of the cakes to their hunting hounds, telling them to *hush, puppy*. Perhaps a more authentic story notes that the cakes were first made in Florida, where fishermen often fried fish outdoors in large pans, attracting dogs who would whine and bark. To quiet the dogs, the cook would fry up some cornmeal cakes and throw them to the dogs, shouting, "Hush, puppies!" *Hush puppies* for soft shoes or slippers seem to have been so named by the first company to manufacture them, in the 1960s.

# I

**IF JESUS WERE ALIVE TODAY HE WOULD BE AT THE SUPER BOWL.** According to *Time* magazine (January 21, 1982) Protestant clergyman and author Norman Vincent Peale, a football fan, made this remark in referring to the 1981 Super Bowl. It has been much quoted since, though rarely if ever used seriously.

**IN A HOLE.** This expression for "in debt or some other kind of trouble" can be traced to gambling houses of the mid–nineteenth century where the proprietors took a certain percentage of each hand for the house. This money, according to a gambling book of the time, was put in the *hole,* which was "a slot cut in the middle of the poker table, leading to a locked drawer underneath, and all checks deposited therein are the property of the keeper of the place." When a person had put all of his money into the poker table hole, he was *in a hole.*

**IN AT THE KILL.** If you consider fox hunting a sport—Oscar Wilde said a fox hunt consisted of "the unspeakable in pursuit of the unedible"—this expression can be considered a sports phrase. *In at the kill* means "participating in the finish of something, especially something satisfying and vindictive," and originated in the upper-crust British world of the hunt sometime during the 1800s. (*See* TALLYHO.)

**INDIANA ACCOLADE.** The common action of banging the cue on the floor in a vertical position to applaud a good shot in a game of pool is called an *Indiana accolade*—possibly because an unknown Indiana player first "applauded" the shot of a rival this way.

**I NEVER MISSED ONE IN MY HEART.** Veteran major-league baseball umpire Bill Klem, who retired in 1941, said this to assure his admirers and detractors that he had never made a call, right or wrong, that he didn't believe was right. The expression is now used by people in and out of sports as a profession of sincerity.

**INFIGHTING.** *Infighting* is a style of fighting at close quarters developed by 160-pound British champion David Mendoza; the term was first recorded in 1816. Since about 1848 *infighting* has also meant fighting among rivals within a group, the expression most often heard as *political infighting.*

**IN HOCK.** In the game of faro, much played by nineteenth-century Americans, the last card in the box was called the *hocketty* or *hock* (from a word of unknown origin). This card was a bad bet, most often a losing one, and *to be in hock* came to mean "to owe money." Since pawnshops were a convenient place to get money to pay debts, they became known as *hock shops,* and *to be in hock* soon meant to have one's valuable possessions in a hock shop or generally to be in very bad financial shape.

**INNING.** (*See* HAVE ONE'S INNINGS.)

**INTESTINAL FORTITUDE.** The head coach of Ohio State University's football team, Dr. John W. Wilce, is said to have invented this phrase for "guts" in 1915 as "a protest against the lurid language of the gridiron and locker room"—*guts* then being considered "improper for drawing room conversation." They don't make coaches like Dr.

Wilce anymore, nor locker rooms so innocent. (*See* LOCKER ROOM TALK.)

**IN THE BAG.** It's usually assumed that this metaphor derives from hunting, where it refers to birds and other small game already safely in the game bag. *Bag* has been used as an abbreviation for *game bag* since at least the fifteenth century, but the expression *in the bag* is first recorded in 1925. William Bancroft Miller, writing in *Verbatim* (February 1977), offers another explanation that attributes the phrase to cockfighting: "Until comparatively recent years, it was common to transport game chickens to the scene of battle in cloth bags rather than in the comfortable and elaborate carrying cases now in vogue, and the roosters were not removed until the fight was about to begin. A cocker, confident of the prowess of his feathered warrior, would say that victory was *in the bag* for him." Neither theory is supported by quotations and neither explains the sinister implication these words often have, for the expression frequently means "rigged" or "fixed."

**IN THE BALLPARK.** (*See* BALLPARK FIGURE.)

**IN THE CLUTCH.** A baseball player who performs well in a critical moment of a game has been called a *clutch player* or *clutch hitter* for over half a century now. The derivation of the term is unclear but the expression is widely used today outside of sports as well. Someone who performs well in any important or crucial situation is said to be dependable or reliable *in the clutch.*

**IN THE HOLE.** (*See* ON DECK.)

**IN THERE PITCHING.** People who try hard and keep working are *in there pitching.* The baseball-derived term suggests a workhorse pitcher doing his best, allowing a hit or walk or run here and there but diligently getting the job done.

Interestingly, the expression is not recorded until the Great Depression, when everyone had to be *in there pitching* to survive. The word *pitcher* in baseball was first recorded in 1854.

**IPICLES.** (*See* AS FAST AS LADAS.)

**IRON MAN.** (*See* LOU GEHRIG'S DISEASE.)

**I SHOULD HAVE STOOD IN BED.** (*See* WE WUZ ROBBED.)

**IT.** (*See* EENY, MEENY, MINY, MO.)

**IT'S ALL OVER BUT THE SHOUTING.** Meaning victory is certain, this expression seems to have appeared in print for the first time in 1842, when a Welsh sportswriter used it. Though the phrase may have originated in sports, it could have its roots in local elections settled by voice vote in rural England. These elections, associated with great noise, came to be called "shoutings." There is no proof of this, but perhaps some candidate or observer of the day was so sure of the outcome of a "shouting" that he remarked *it's all over but the shouting* and the phrase passed into popular usage.

**IT'S A NEW BALL GAME.** Since about 1940, Americans have been using this catch phrase to mean "What's past is past, we start over from here." The saying almost certainly has its origins in baseball and sounds like something a baseball announcer may have spontaneously invented when a game was suddenly tied up. The expression is often *it's a whole new ball game.* (*See* THAT'S THE BALLGAME.)

**IT'S HOW YOU PLAYED THE GAME.** Sportswriter Grantland Rice, who coined the term the "Four Horsemen" to describe Notre Dame's famous backfield in an account of a Notre Dame–Army game ("Outlined against a blue-gray

October sky, the Four Horsemen rode again''), is also responsible for *it's how you played the game.* The much loved writer, who died in 1954 at the age of seventy-three, first used the expression in a poem he published in one of his ''The Sportlight'' columns:

*When One Great Scorer comes*
*To mark against your name,*
*He writes—not that you won or lost—*
*But how you played the game.*

(*See* FOUR HORSEMEN; RETIRING A NUMBER; WINNING ISN'T EVERYTHING.)

**IT'S NOT CRICKET.** (*See* CRICKET.)

**IT'S THE ONLY BALLGAME IN TOWN.** (*See* THAT'S THE BALLGAME.)

**IVY LEAGUE.** The colleges referred to as the *Ivy League* are Harvard, Yale, Princeton, Dartmouth, Cornell, Brown, Columbia and the University of Pennsylvania. They are all old-line institutions, with thick-vined, aged ivy covering their walls, and the designation at first applied specifically to their football teams. Sportswriter Caswell Adams coined the term in the mid-thirties. At the time, Fordham University's football team was among the best in the East. A fellow journalist compared Columbia and Princeton to Fordham, and Adams replied, ''Oh they're just Ivy League,'' recalling later that he said this ''with complete humorous disparagement in mind.''

# J

**JACK ARMSTRONG, THE ALL-AMERICAN BOY.** Every red-blooded American boy ate his Wheaties, the Breakfast of Champions, during the 1930s and '40s, thanks in large part to Jack Armstrong, The All-American Boy. "Jack Armstrong the All-American Boy" was a radio serial presented afternoons, right after school, by Wheaties. Many believe the eponymous hero's name was suggested by the real-life bully Jack Armstrong, who lost a legendary wrestling match with young Abe Lincoln and later became his friend. Actually, General Mills (Wheaties) executive Sammy Gale had roomed with an athlete named Jack Armstrong in college and decided to use his name for the program's hero because it seemed to convey "all-American virtues of courage, a sense of humor, and the championing of ideals." Jack Lawrence Armstrong, the model for Jack Armstrong, was the son of a retired British Army officer who moved to the United States from Canada at the age of four and later received a civil engineering degree from the University of Minnesota. He was a much-decorated Army Air Force officer during World War II and later served on the Atomic Energy Commission and worked for the Apollo and Gemini space programs. He died in 1985, aged seventy-four.

**JACK DEMPSEY.** This Amazonian fish named after former world heavyweight champion Jack Dempsey (1895–1983) is described by scientists as "a very aggressive species," which is no doubt the reason for its popular name.

**JACK JOHNSON.** John Arthur ("Jack") Johnson, his memory recently revived by the play *The Great White Hope,* loudly proclaimed that he reigned as the first black world heavyweight champion in 1908 when he KO'd Englishman Tommy Burns—though his title claim was disputed and not settled until he demolished Jim Jeffries, the original *great white hope,* in 1910. Johnson held the title until 1915, when giant Jess Willard knocked him out in twenty-six rounds in Havana, Cuba. The American fighter had often been called the "Big Smoke" in the United States, "smoke" being common slang at the time for "Negro." For this reason, and because he was so powerful a man, the German 5.9 howitzer, its shell and its shell burst were named after Johnson. A formidable weapon, whose shells emitted thick black smoke upon exploding, the *Jack Johnson* saw action against the Allies during World War I, when Johnson's name was prominent in the news for his fights and love affairs; the boxer, in fact, had fled to Europe in 1913 after being convicted of violating the Mann Act, unjustly or not. It is said that Johnson's name may be the source of the slang term *Johnson* for the penis, but this derivation is not certain. The great fighter died in 1946, at age sixty-eight.

**JACKPOT.** The source of this synonym for a big win isn't the slot machine that pays out jackpots. The metaphor has its origin in the variety of draw poker called "jacks or better," in which only a pair of jacks or a better hand can open the betting. Players ante up into the pot before each deal and it often takes a large number of deals before one player is dealt a pair of jacks or a better hand. By that time the "progressive jack pot" has mounted up to a large sum, or a considerable *jackpot,* for the player who wins it. From poker, the word *jackpot* passed into general use, first recorded in a nonpoker sense in 1884. It was subsequently used in phrases like *to hit the jackpot,* "to have great luck," first recorded in 1944.

**JACK ROBINSON.** Contrary to popular belief, the saying *as quick as you can say Jack Robinson* has no connection with Jackie Robinson, the first black major league baseball player, though Jackie Robinson was quick enough to beat out many a bunt and steal many a base. Notable attempts have been made to trace this eighteenth-century British phrase, all unsuccessful. One popular explanation has the saying's origin in the habit a certain Jack Robinson had of paying extraordinarily quick visits to his friends, the gentleman leaving even before his name could be announced. But *Jack Robinson* was probably used in the phrase simply because it is a very common name in England and is easy to pronounce.

**JACKSON HAINES.** The well known sitting-spin of figure skating is called the *Jackson Haines,* after American skater Jackson Haines (1840–1879), a former dancer who was largely responsible for creating modern figure skating by applying dance techniques to the sport.

**JAI ALAI.** The name for this court game is Basque in origin, formed from the Basque *jai,* "festival," and *alai,* "joyous," indicating that people have always had a good time playing *jai alai.* Other English words that come from the Basque include *bizarre* and *orignal,* a mostly Canadian word for the American moose.

**JEOPARDY.** *Jeu parti* was originally a French chess term meaning "a divided play or game." It thus came to mean "an uncertain chance, uncertainty" and entered English in this sense, spelled *jeuparti,* early in the thirteenth century. By the end of that century it had attained its present meaning of "risk of loss; peril, danger," but its spelling is not recorded as *jeopardy* until 1597. Today a popular quiz show is named "Jeopardy!"

**JIM DANDY.** No particular Jim Dandy seems to be the eponym behind the century-old term *Jim Dandy,* which is still heard for someone or something that is especially fine or admirable. *The Dictionary of Americanisms* traces the term back to January 1887, but not in a sports context. Etymologist Gerald Cohen has cited a published sports usage of it some six months later in a New York Giants game, indicating a possible baseball origin. Certainly baseball helped popularize the phrase.

**JINX.** Baseball Hall of Famer Christy Mathewson was among the first to use this word in print when he wrote in his *Pitching in a Pinch* (1912): "A jinx is something which brings bad luck to a ballplayer." Big Six probably didn't know that the word may owe its life to a bird called the *jynx,* which was used to cast charms and spells. The *jynx,* known in America as the wrynecked woodpecker or wryneck, takes its name from the Greek *iynx* for the bird. In the Middle Ages this rara avis, with its grotesque, twisted neck, its odd breeding and feeding habits, its harsh, strident cries during migration and its near silence the rest of the time, was thought to have occult powers. As jynx feathers were used to make love potions and black-magic charms, the bird's name itself came to mean a charm or spell, especially a black-magic spell, cast on a selected victim. It's easy to see how the slang term *jinx* arose from *jynx,* but the long flight of the jynx from medieval times to the printed page of 1912 is not easily explained.

**JOCK.** Beginning in the late 1960s, a *jock* meant a big, brainless college football player. *Jock* is a kinder word today covering any athlete at all. No one knows if the term is directly related to the racing *jockey* or to the *jockstrap* most male athletes wear, although the latter derivation seems more plausible. *Jockstrap* takes its name from the centuries-old English slang *jock* for "penis," which derived from the common nickname *Jock* for John; the word is first recorded in a 1919 ad for "Schnoter's Suspensories and Jock Straps."

**JOCK ITCH.** (*See* ATHLETE'S FOOT.)

**JOCKSTRAP.** (*See* JOCK.)

**JOE LOUIS.** Perhaps the greatest of all heavyweight fighters, Joe Louis came to be nicknamed the Brown Bomber for the color of his skin and his explosive right. Born Joe Louis Barrow on May 13, 1914, in Lafayette, Alabama, he was the son of a sharecropper who died when Joe was four years old. The family eventually moved to Detroit, where Joe helped support them by taking odd jobs that included work as a sparring partner in a local gym. This led him to a boxing career in which he took the heavyweight title from Jim Braddock in 1937. Joe Louis defended his title more often than any other champion in ring history, and only Jack Dempsey outpolled him in a 1959 Associated Press survey in which sportswriters picked the best boxers of the century. Louis lost three times in his career (which was interrupted by service in World War II): once before he became champion to Max Schmeling, whom he knocked out in a rematch; then to Rocky Marciano and Ezzard Charles when he was attempting a comeback after retiring as the undefeated heavyweight champion. His ring record was sixty-four KO's, eight decisions, and one win by default. A *Joe Louis* has become synonymous for the best fighter, a heavyweight without peer.

**JUDO.** *Judo* means "the gentle way" in Japanese. It is a modern variation of the ancient sport of *ji-jitsu* first played by samurai. *Judo* was invented around 1882 by Japanese educator Jigoro Kano, who was appalled with the violence used by many of his countrymen practicing ji-jitsu. Kano outlawed many dangerous moves of the older sport, including foot strikes, and developed several new moves. The sport quickly caught on in Japan and other countries, including the United States, where Teddy Roosevelt became a devotee.

**JUMPING THE GUN.** This expression for acting too quickly has been commonly used since the early 1900s. From track and field, the phrase is suggested by a runner who jumps off the starting line before the gun is fired to begin the race.

**JUST FOR OPENERS.** Originally a poker term dating back to the early nineteenth century, and strictly meaning someone's first bet in a game, *just for openers* was quickly adopted into other realms. In the business world it is still frequently used to mean someone's first offer or action.

**JUST IN THE NICK OF TIME.** In early days, scores in many games were recorded by scoring notches, or nicks, on a stick called a tally. Any last-minute score was called *a nick in time* and this expression, altered to *in the nick of time* or *just in the nick of time,* came to mean "not a second too soon." (*See* SCORE.)

**JUST UNDER THE WIRE.** This phrase means to barely make the limit or meet the deadline. The expression is from horse racing, where the imaginary "wire" is the finish line and a horse just under the wire is one who beats out another horse by a nose to finish in the money.

**KAPUT.** In the old French gambling game of piquet, *capot* meant not to win a single trick. *Capot* became the German *kaputt,* with the same meaning, which over a long period of time was extended to mean "having been destroyed, wrecked, or incapacitated," just as some players would be after not winning a single trick in a game. By the end of the nineteenth century *kaputt* had entered English as *kaput.*

**KARATE.** Born in China and refined in Japan, *karate* is the ancient art of defending oneself against an armed attacker by striking sensitive areas on the attacker's body with the hands, elbows, knees or feet. Centuries later the sport of karate based on this method of self-defense was introduced. Modern karate owes much to Japanese karate master Funakoshi Gichin, who taught the art and indeed gave it the name *karate,* from the Japanese *kara,* "empty," and *te,* "hands." *Shotokan karate* (named after Funakoshi's nickname, Shoto) is the most popular form of karate today. (*See* KUNG FU.)

**KEEP ONE'S END UP.** (*See* HAVE ONE'S INNINGS.)

**KEEP THE BALL ROLLING.** The election of 1840, which pitted incumbent President Martin Van Buren against General William Henry Harrison, a legendary hero who fought against the Indians at Tippecanoe, and Virginian John Tyler, brought with it the first modern political campaign.

Some historians believe that the election gave us the expression *keep the ball rolling* as well as the term *OK.* One popular advertising stunt that helped Harrison win over "Tippecanoe and Tyler, too" was "to keep the ball rolling" for "the log cabin and hard cider candidate." Ten-foot "victory balls," made of tin and leather and imprinted with the candidate's name, were rolled from city to city for hundreds of miles. While these victory balls did popularize the expression *keep the ball rolling*—keep interest from flagging—the saying undoubtedly dates back to the late eighteenth century. Of British origin, it alludes to either the game of bandy (a form of hockey where the puck is a small ball) or the game of rugby. In either sport the game isn't interesting unless the ball is rolling. The first form of the expression was *keep the ball up.*

**KEEP YOUR EYE ON THE BALL.** Many sports could have spawned this Americanism meaning "be closely attentive." Baseball, tennis, golf and basketball are all candidates, but the saying seems to have derived from the exhortations of college football coaches to their charges at the turn of the century. *To be on the ball,* to be vitally alert or in the know, is apparently an offshoot of this phrase; in baseball it can be said of a pitcher who has a wide variety of effective pitches.

**KEEP YOUR PECKER UP.** *Keep your pecker up* is a British expression from the early nineteenth century and the *pecker* in it means "spirits." The phrase is infrequently heard in the United States, undoubtedly due to the slang use of pecker for "penis," but it is an exhortation for someone to keep his courage or chin up. It probably comes from the "sport" of cockfighting, where a *pecker* is a bird's beak. When a gamecock's beak droops it indicates he is tired and close to defeat.

**KELLY POOL.** This is a variety of pool in which each player draws a number; while trying to sink the balls in numerical order, the players must pocket their numbered balls as well. It is said to be named for an unknown Irishman surnamed Kelly, or in honor of Ireland, where it was invented.

**KENTUCKY DERBY.** (*See* DERBY.)

**"K" FOR A STRIKEOUT.** The practice of using the letter *K* for a strikeout dates back as far as 1861. In those days, when a hitter struck out, it was said that "he struck." Letters were used for scoring, as they are today: *E* for an error, *S* for a sacrifice, etc. Since the letter *S* could not also be used for "struck," the last letter, *K* of the word "struck" was used, and it has remained the symbol for a strikeout. Henry Chadwick, the newspaperman credited with inventing the box score, invented all these symbols, the term *K* used at first "for a player who missed the ball in three swings."

**KIBITZER.** It seems that German card players of the sixteenth century found meddlesome onlookers just as annoying as do today's card players. The constant gratuitous "advice" of these chatterers reminded them of the *kiebitz* (the lapwing, or plover) whose shrill cries frighten game away from approaching hunters. Thus all *kibitzers* are named for this troublesome bird, our peewit, which inspired the German word *kiebitzen,* "to look on at cards."

**KICKOFF.** Today, to *kickoff* an event means to start it. The phrase has obviously been influenced by American football, where the *kickoff* is the beginning of the game, but it more likely comes from soccer, in which there is a similar *kickoff. Kickoff* is first recorded in 1855, long before the first American football game.

**KILLER INSTINCT.** It is said that when former heavyweight champion Jack Dempsey fought, all he thought about was killing his opponent. True or not, the expression *killer instinct* seems to have been coined in the 1920s after Dempsey's beatings of Jess Willard, Georges Carpentier and Luis Firpo. From boxing, the term was extended to all areas of life, although no major dictionary records this very common expression. (*See* JACK DEMPSEY.)

**KILL THE UMP.** Umpires were often the targets of rocks, pop bottles and ripe tomatoes in the early days of baseball, and they were frequently assaulted on and off the field by players and fans. Things got so bad that it was suggested that umpires be suspended in protective cages over the field. Fans of the day, much as those of today, claimed that umpires couldn't see a foot in front of them, as illustrated by the following ditty written in 1868: "Breathes there a fan with soul so dead/ Who never to the ump hath said:/ Yer blind, you bum!" This charge so infuriated National League President Thomas Lynch, a former umpire, that in 1911 he had a committee of oculists test the vision of all the umpires in the league. The committee reported that every umpire had 20/20 corrected vision or better.

But was *kill the ump* ever more than an idle threat? Several minor league umpires did indeed lose their lives on the diamond over close calls. And in 1911, Patrick Casey, a convicted murderer at Nevada State Penitentiary, was granted the customary last request. Casey wanted to umpire a baseball game before he died, so a game was arranged on the prison grounds and he was named umpire. When the game ended, he was executed. (*See* BLIND TOM; UMPIRE.)

**KITTY.** Willard Espy offers the following explanation for *kitty,* the pot to which poker players contribute, in *Thou Improper, Thou Uncommon Noun* (1978): "[The name] Catherine turned to Kate, and Kate to Kitty. Some Kittys were no better than they should be, and Kitty became one of the many epithets applied to prostitutes. Spirited Johns—not yet lowercased for a prostitute's customer—used to amuse themselves by tossing coins into the laps of Kittys, as poker players today throw their antes or bets into a kitty in the hope of getting a winning hand. The sequence cannot be proved—no one will talk—but it seems plausible." Note that no cats are involved in this tale.

**KLONDIKE.** (*See* CANFIELD.)

**KNOCK DOWN, DRAG OUT FIGHT.** This expression for a rough, anything-goes fight is first recorded in 1827 British boxing circles, before there were many rules governing prizefighting.

**KNOCK THE SPOTS OFF.** The origins of this Americanism for "to defeat decisively" are not clear, but some FBE (Federal Bureau of Etymology) agents believe it is from the world of boxing. Word sleuths reason that the expression is first recorded in a sports story and—admittedly reaching on this one—speculate that the spots in question were freckles figuratively knocked off the face of a badly beaten fighter. However, the expression could have its roots in the sharpshooting of nineteenth-century American marksmen, who could shoot the pips (or spots) out of a playing card nailed to a tree a considerable distance away.

**KNUCKLE DOWN.** Marble players may be credited for this expression, which dates back to seventeeth-century England. One rule in the game provides that a player must shoot directly from the spot where his or her marble lands; this requires that the player *knuckle down,* that is, put his knuckles on the ground. Since marbles was a popular pastime with adults as well as children at the time, *knuckle down* possibly came to express earnest application to any job. However, the bones of the spinal column were also known as "knuckles" in the seventeenth century, and the expression may derive from the act of "putting one's back into a task."

**KUNG FU.** Historians tell us that there is little positive evidence of the Chinese philosopher's existence, but it is said that the Chinese K'ung clan, descendants of Confucius, numbers over fifty thousand today and that Confucius's burial place outside Kufow is still a place of homage. Confucius is the Latinized form of the philosopher's name, K'ung Fu-tzu ("philosopher" or "master K'ung"), which may be the origin of the oriental martial art *kung fu,* although no hard evidence supports this theory. Believed to have been born around 551 B.C. of a poor but noble family, Confucius taught and held a number of government posts. By his death when he was seventy-two, the philosopher had attracted some three thousand disciples who helped spread his ethical teachings, which were based primarily on his "golden rule": "What you do not like when done to yourself do not do to others." (*See* KARATE.)

# L

**LACROSSE.** *Lacrosse* is probably the only sport whose name has religious significance. When French priest Pierre de Charlevoix saw Algonquin Indians playing their game of *baggataway* in 1705, he thought that the webbed sticks they used resembled a bishop's cross and called the game *lacrosse,* "the cross," the name which eventually supplanted the Indian one. An historic *lacrosse* game was played on June 4, 1763. While playing "to celebrate George III's birthday," Obijway and Sac Indians propelled the ball over the walls of Fort Muchillimackinae, rushed in on the pretext of retrieving it, seized weapons hidden by their squaws and massacred the garrison.

**LARK.** *Larking* was a popular sport in the sixteenth and seventeenth century, when groups of young men and women took nets into the woods and fields to catch meadowlarks, a gamebird then highly esteemed for the table. Great fun was had on these *larks,* by all except the birds, and soon the word *lark* was being used to mean any frolic or good time.

**LAST LICKS.** Since at least 1883, *last licks* has meant a team's last three outs in baseball, its last chance to win the game. It has since come to mean anyone's last try at anything. *To put in one's best licks* means to make a winning effort and, although this term dates back to the 1700s and is of unclear origin, the baseball connection has kept it alive.

**LAUGHER.** A game in any sport in which one side wins by a huge margin is called a *laugher,* because such a lopsided victory is a laughing matter (at least to the winning team). The expression may have originated in baseball.

**LAY AN EGG.** Comedians and other entertainers *lay an egg* when their acts fail, but the phrase originated in the sports world, not in show business. Stranger still, the expression comes from the sport of cricket, England's national game. *Duck's egg* was British slang for "no score" in cricket for many years, and in about 1860 the expression *achieved a duck's egg* was used to describe a team that hadn't scored and had only large oval zeroes shaped like duck's eggs on the scoreboard. Ten years later the phrase became more expressive as *laid a duck's egg* and this came into American baseball slang as *laid a goose egg.* In baseball the expression for zero soon became just *goose eggs,* and it still is, but early vaudevillians adopted the expression and changed it to *laid an egg.* (*See* CRICKET.)

**LEAD WITH YOUR CHIN.** The allusion here is to boxing, where a fighter who doesn't protect himself with a right- or left-handed lead, but sticks his chin out to lead, is risking a knockout blow. *Leading with your chin* or "sticking your chin out" has been slang for taking a big chance since the 1920s, while "taking it on the chin" has meant to suffer severe failure since about the same time. The expression *take it,* as in "He can really take it" (handle adversity), is probably a descendant of *take it on the chin.*

**LEAVE IN THE LURCH.** *Lourche,* or "lurch," was an old French dicing game resembling backgammon that was popular in the sixteenth century. Any player who incurred a lurch in the game was left helplessly behind the goal—so far behind his opponent that he couldn't possibly win—which led to the figurative meaning of leaving someone in a helpless plight. The expression persists in English despite the fact that no one plays the old dicing game anymore, possibly because *lurch* describes a similar position in the game of cribbage.

**LEOTARDS.** We owe this word to nineteenth-century French aerialist Jules Leotard, who claimed in his *Memoirs* to have invented the outfit still worn by circus performers and gymnasts. Originally the costume was a one-piece elastic garment, snug-fitting and low at the neck and sleeveless. Leotard, born to the circus—when he was a baby, his aerialist parents would hang him upside-down from a trapeze bar to stop his crying—intended his costume for men, not women. "Do you want to be adored by the ladies?" he exhorts his male readers in his *Memoirs*. "[Then] put on a more natural garb, which does not hide your best features!" (*See* ACROBAT.)

**LETTER.** (*See* FOUR LETTER MAN.)

**LIGHTWEIGHT.** British boxers who weighed under 154 pounds were called *lightweights* as early as 1850, although the American lightweight division today is 127–135 pounds. Before that, in the 1730s, *lightweight* had been used in English horse racing to refer to lightweight gentlemen riders. Both of these terms were the inspiration for the general expression *lightweight,* meaning an unimportant or inconsequential person, which is first recorded in 1882. *Flyweight, bantamweight* and *featherweight* are lighter divisions in boxing than *lightweight,* but only *featherweight* has much use as a derogatory term. (*See* HEAVYWEIGHT.)

**LOCKER ROOM TALK.** This term refers to the vulgar, lewd or obscene language men (and maybe even women) are thought to speak in locker rooms, although some locker rooms are more staid than others. It's a good guess that this expression doesn't go back beyond the 1940s, but no one knows for sure.

**LOLLIPOP.** Is the *lollipop* named after a racehorse? The story goes that in the early 1900s one George Smith, a Connecticut candy manufacturer, "put together the candy and the stick" and named it in honor of Lolly Pop, the era's most famous racehorse. The name *lollipop* then became a trademarked name used by the Bradley-Smith Company of New Haven. It is true that candy on a stick wasn't known in America before about 1908, and neither was the word *lollipop.* Smith may have invented the confection (there are no other claimants) and he may have even named his candy on a stick after the horse in question. But the word *lollipop,* for a piece of sucking candy that dissolves easily in the mouth (*not* one, however, that is attached to a stick) was widely used in England as early as the late eighteenth century. It apparently derives from the English dialect word *lolly,* used in northern England to mean "tongue," plus the word *pop,* in reference to the sound children made when sucking the candy. Somehow the lollipop remained unknown to Americans until the candy on a stick was manufactured in the early twentieth century, but this is not to say that the racehorse Lolly Pop couldn't have been named for the earlier British term.

**LONG SHOT.** With a six-foot English longbow made of seasoned heart of red yew, which was so valued at the time that it was protected as a war material, a skilled archer could shoot as far as four hundred yards. From the time of William the Conqueror, archery was encouraged by English rulers and every adult male was required to own a longbow; in village archery contests every man strove to set a village record with the most accurate long shot. Thus *long shot* may have entered general speech as a synonym for any unusual or improbable feat, from a long archery shot that hit the mark dead center to a horse that won a race against great odds. (*See* NOT BY A LONG SHOT.)

**LOU GEHRIG'S DISEASE.** The fatal paralytic disease amyotrophic lateral sclerosis has had this name since Yankee first baseman Lou Gehrig died of it in 1941. Known as the Iron Man, the Iron Horse and the Crown Prince (to Babe Ruth) of Swat, Gehrig played in 2,130 consecutive games for the Yankees before the disease took its toll.

**LOUISVILLE SLUGGER.** The largest city in Kentucky, Louisville was named in 1780 for France's Louis XVI in recognition of the assistance he had given to America during the Revolutionary War. Home of Fort Knox, the Kentucky Derby, the mint julep and many bourbon distilleries, Louisville also houses the famous Hillerich & Bradsby's baseball bat factory, where the renowned *Louisville Slugger* has been made since 1884. The bat is, of course, named after the city named after a king. *Louisville Sluggers* are made from prime white ash; one mature tree makes sixty bats and more than 6 million are turned out each year. Some 2 percent of the annual production goes to professional ballplayers, these fashioned from specifications noted in a fifty-thousand-card file covering the bat preferences of ballplayers past and present.

**LOVE.** A person who fails to score in tennis might be said to be playing for the love of the game. According to this theory, which is widely supported, *love* for "zero in tennis" comes from the expression "play for the money or play for love" (nothing). The idea here is similar to that behind the word *amateur,* which comes from the Latin *amare,* "to love," and strictly speaking means a person who loves a game or subject. But there is another explanation for the term *love* in tennis, an expression used since at least 1742. *Love* for *goose egg,* or "nothing," may have been born when the English imported the game of tennis from France. Because a zero resembles an egg, the French used the expression *l'oeuf,* "egg," for "no score." English players mispronouncing the French expression may have gradually changed it to *love.* (*See* AMATEUR; LAY AN EGG.)

# M

**MAJOR LEAGUE.** The baseball terms *major league* and *minor league* date back to 1882, when the National League was called the major league and the American Association (not today's American League) was called the minor league. Later these two leagues merged and the unified teams became known as the *major leagues,* any league below them being called a minor league. Today, of course, the Major Leagues are composed of the American and National Leagues, each with two divisions. Because the Major Leagues are the highest level of professional baseball, the term *major league* has generally come to mean the best of anything. *Big league,* a synonym, also comes from baseball where it was used as early as 1899.

**MAKE FUR FLY.** The cruel "sport" of capturing raccoons and setting dogs on them (to see how long the coons could last) may have suggested this expression to American pioneers. Certainly the air was filled with fur during such fights and by 1825 *to make fur fly* meant "to attack violently." In the autobiographical *A Narrative of the Life of David Crockett, of the State of Tennessee* (1834) we read: "I knew very well that I was in the devil of a hobble, for my father had been taking a few horns, and was in a good condition to make the fur fly."

**MAKE ONE'S GORGE RISE.** Hunting falcons are fierce, gluttonous creatures that store the food they eat in a pouch called the crop, or gorge. Their trainers in medieval times noticed that they frequently overate and vomited part of their food, which came to be called *gorge* after the pouch it came from. To *make one's gorge rise,* therefore, became a synonym for "to make someone sick." The saying at first indicated extreme disgust and later expressed strong resentment, so that today the phrase means to make a person violently angry.

**MAKE WAVES.** Team players in any sport usually don't *make waves,* that is, they don't make trouble, and the expression might come from sculling, in which a rower's strokes must be smooth and uniform, not choppy. But the phrase might be from the old joke about a person who arrives in hell and hears the place filled with lovely serene voices singing, though he can't make out the words. Amazed at such peace and serenity in the nether regions, he approaches closer only to find the chorus of hell standing up to their chins in excrement, singing endlessly to each other, softly, serenely, carefully, *"Don't make waves, don't make waves."*

**MAKING THE HORN.** The Greek hunter Actaeon came upon Artemis bathing and—either because he saw her naked or because he had boasted that he was a better hunter than she—the goddess of wildlife (called Diana in Roman mythology) changed him into a stag and he was torn to pieces by his own hounds. Because he had had horns—at least for a short time—the hunter Actaeon's name became a synonym for a man with an unfaithful wife. In fact, *to actaeon,* now obsolete, was once a verb meaning "to cuckold." No one really knows why horns are a symbol of cuckoldry, but one guess is that stags, which are of course horned, have their harems taken from them in the rutting season by stronger males. At any rate, *making the horn*—thrusting out a fist with the first and last fingers extended—has been a gesture of contempt, implying a person is a cuckold, since Roman times.

**MALL.** Even our word for a shopping *mall* has a sports derivation. The word comes directly from the shaded walks in parks called *malls,* which in turn took their name from the alleys in these parks called *pall-malls* on which a croquet-like game of *pall-mall* was played beginning in the sixteenth century. The game itself was named from the Italian *palla,* ball, and *maglio,* mallet.

**MARATHON.** This grueling 26-mile, 365-yard footrace honors a peerless runner but is named after a prosaic vegetable. It recalls the historic battle of Marathon; *Marathon* means "field of fennel" in Greek, the word deriving from the Greek *marathron,* a fennel plant. In 490 B.C. on the great plain of Marathon covered with this yellow-flowered plant, twenty thousand invading Persians tried to establish a beachhead and defeat the armies of the Greek city states before launching an assault on Athens itself. Led by General Datis, the Persians were under the orders of their King Darius to enslave Athens and "bring the slaves into his presence." Legend has it that the Greek soldier Pheidippides, a champion of the old Olympic games and the best runner in Greece, was dispatched from Athens to Sparta to announce the arrival of the invading Persians at Marathon and seek a promise of help. Pheidippides covered the distance of 150 miles over mountain trails in two days, only to find that the Spartans were unwilling to send help until after the conclusion of an ongoing religious festival. He then ran back to join his forces in the defense of Athens. Although the bronze-clad Greeks were outnumbered two to one, their commander Miltiades employed revolutionary tactics to defeat the Persians on the marshy plain near Marathon village.

**MASCOT.** *Mascots,* animals that are adopted as good luck symbols for sports teams, take their name from the French word *mascotte,* meaning "good luck charm." The word is first recorded in English in 1881 at about the time the French opera *La Mascotte* was being performed in Europe.

**MASHIE.** Golf's number five iron may take its (now rarely heard) name from the way unskilled golfers "mashed" a ball with it. Or it may have resembled some Scottish kitchen utensil used to mash potatoes around the time the club was introduced in 1888. But more likely it derives from the French word for club, *massue.*

**MATADOR.** (*See* TOREADOR.)

**MERCURY.** (*See* AS FAST AS LADAS.)

**MIDSUMMER DREAM GAME.** (*See* ALL-STAR.)

**MINIATURE GOLF.** (*See* TOM THUMB GOLF.)

**MINOR LEAGUE.** (*See* MAJOR LEAGUE.)

**MONDAY MORNING QUARTERBACK.** Someone who plans strategies or criticizes the actions of others with the benefit of hindsight and not in the heat of battle is a *Monday morning quarterback.* The Americanism is from football, dating back to the early 1940s, and originally referred to the fervid fan who tells anyone who will listen on Monday morning just what the quarterback in Saturday's or Sunday's game should have done.

**MORA.** Deriving from the Italian *mora* (of unknown origin), *mora* or *morra* is a game in which one player guesses the number of fingers held up by another player. The ancient Romans called the game *micare digitis* and a Chinese version is called *chai mei.* The game, almost identical to a game called "love," was recorded in England about a century earlier (1585); a player in this version holds up a certain number of fingers and the other player, with eyes closed, tries to guess that number. The old game was played by Rabelais and, no doubt, Shakespeare.

**MORGAN HORSE.** Justin Morgan is the only American horse ever to sire a distinctive breed. A bay stallion foaled in about 1793, he belonged to Justin Morgan (1747–1798), a Vermont schoolteacher. The horse bearing Morgan's name was probably a blend of thoroughbred and Arabian, fairly small at fourteen hands high and weighing eight hundred pounds. Morgan, an aspiring musician, bought his colt in Massachusetts, naming him Figure and training him so well that he won trotting races against much larger thoroughbreds. Eventually, with success, Figure came to be called after his master. After his owner died, Justin Morgan was bought and sold many times in the twenty-eight years of his life. One of those unusual horses whose dominant traits persist despite centuries of inbreeding, his individual characteristics remain essentially unchanged in the *Morgan* breed of horses he sired. *Morgans* are still compact, virile horses noted for their intelligence, docility and longevity and many of them are still active when thirty years of age or more. Heavy-shouldered, with a short neck but delicate head, they are noted for their airy carriage and naturally pure gait and speed. *Morgans* were long the favorite breed for American trotters until the Hambletonian strain replaced them.

**MORNING GLORY.** Because the *Morning Glory* only opens its flowers in the morning, it has been used as a synonym in sports and elsewhere for a person who begins brilliantly but soon starts to fade, not fulfilling his or her promise. The expression dates back almost a century in American sports.

**MUFF.** Not much used today, a *muff* is a thick tubular case for the hands that is covered with fur and used mostly by women to keep their hands warm. Around the turn of the century, the word was first used to describe a baseball player who misses an easy catch, one who makes a play as if his hands were in a *muff.*

**MULLIGAN.** When you're allowed to take a *mulligan* in golf—a free shot not counted against the score after your first one goes bad—you may not be emulating some duffer of days gone by. *Mulligan* probably comes from the brand name of a once-popular sauce that was standard in barrooms. This potent seasoning of water and hot pepper seeds was sometimes mixed with beer and jokers swore that it ate out your liver, stomach and finally your heart—which is just what happens when you accept too many *mulligans* on the golf course. On the other hand, there are those who say that *mulligan* derives from the name of Canadian David Mulligan, who in the late 1920s was allowed an extra shot by his friends in appreciation for driving them over rough roads every week for their foursome at the St. Lambert Country Club near Montreal. Needless to say, the former story is more popular.

**MUTT AND JEFF.** We frequently use this expression to describe two friends, one is short and one tall. The term is from the comic strip *Mutt and Jeff,* created by Henry Conway (Bud) Fisher in 1907, but the little guy is named after former heavyweight champion James J. Jeffries. This happened when artist Fisher had Augustus Mutt, the tall, chinless member of the duo, visit a sanitarium in an early strip; there Mutt met a pleasant little inmate who fancied himself the boxing great Jim Jeffries. Mutt dubbed him Jeff for this reason. Jeffries (1875–1953) was one of the few heavyweight champions to retire undefeated, but just as Joe Louis was KO'd when he made a comeback, so was Jeffries—by Jack Johnson in 1910.

# N

**NAPOLEON.** *Napoleon* is a card game in which the players bid for the privilege of naming the trump by stating the number of tricks they propose to win. It was named for Napoleon Bonaparte in about 1810. A variation of the game is *Wellington,* named after Napoleon's great adversary, the Duke of Wellington.

**NASSAU.** In a golf game, a *Nassau* is an eighteen-hole match in which one point each is given to the players having the lowest scores for the first nine holes, the second nine holes and the entire round. The scoring and betting system is not named for the seaport capital of Nassau in the Bahamas, as is often said. It is actually named after the Nassau County Golf Course at Glen Cove in Nassau County, Long Island, New York, where it was developed in 1901 by players who didn't want to lose by embarrassingly high scores.

**NATIONAL PASTIME.** Baseball was becoming a truly *national game* in about 1856, when the expression is first recorded, but at that time the term really meant baseball as played by a new code of rules introduced by the New York Knickerbocker Ball Club in 1845. As the game grew even more popular, people assumed that *the national game* meant baseball was the nation's favorite sport and it was used this way; the variation *the national pastime* was introduced in the 1920s.

**NAUMACHIA.** Roman emperors held ''sea battles'' on land in the *Naumachia* (from the Greek for ''sea battle''), a flooded amphitheater Augustus built on the right bank of the Tiber River. The combatants in the two opposing fleets, who were usually prisoners or criminals, fought to the death unless spared by the emperor. As many as twenty-four triremes fought in these bloody contests.

**NECK AND NECK.** Since the late eighteenth or early nineteenth century, this British turf term for a close horse race has been commonly used to describe any race or contest that is virtually tied or even. (*See* DEAD HEAT; NIP AND TUCK.)

**NEUROBAT.** (*See* ACROBAT.)

**NEVER UP, NEVER IN.** Its sexual implications have helped this golfing expression last since the early 1920s as a catch phrase of pessimism. It means, literally, never up near the hole with the first putt, never in the hole with the second putt.

**NICE GUYS FINISH LAST.** This cynical proverb has been attributed by *Bartlett's* to former Brooklyn Dodger manager Leo Durocher, who wrote a book using it as the title. Back in the 1940s Leo was sitting on the bench before a game with the New York Giants and saw opposing manager Mel Ott across the field. ''Look at Ott,'' he said to a group of sportswriters. ''He's such a nice guy and they'll finish last for him.'' One of the writers probably coined the phrase *nice guys finish last* from this remark, but the credit for it still goes to Leo The Lip. It is one of several baseball expressions that have become proverbial outside the sport.

**NICKEL CURVE.** In baseball a *nickel curve* is a curve that doesn't break much and is easy to hit. It is a derogatory term that dates back to 1932. *Curveball* itself has been traced to William Arthur (''Candy'') Cummings (1848–1924), a Hall of Famer who is credited with inventing the curveball over 120 years ago. Cumming's curve was inspired by the half clam shells that he skimmed across a Brooklyn beach as a youngster, but he perfected it by experimenting with a baseball that he bought for a nickel.

**NIMROD.** In the Bible, Nimrod is the son of Cush and the founder of Babel. He may have been an Assyrian king who built the city of Nineveh, the capital of the Assyrian empire. According to scripture, Nimrod was "a mighty hunter before the Lord," and historians tell us that the Assyrian kings were noted for their prowess in hunting. Aramaic translations of the Old Testament say "that mighty hunter before the Lord" means "sinful hunter of the sons of men," which accounts for Pope's and Milton's descriptions of Nimrod as "a mighty hunter, and his prey was man." But a *Nimrod* is more generally the nickname for a great, daring, and skillful hunter, or even sportsman.

**NINE.** *Nine* is obviously a synonym for a baseball team because that's the number of players on a team. But the first recorded use of the word *nine* in this sense is in the name of a team called the New York Nine, which played against the New York Knickerbockers Ball Club in 1846. Thus the term *nine* may derive from the name of a specific team.

**NINETEENTH HOLE.** H. L. Mencken calls *the nineteenth hole* "the one American contribution to the argot of golf." While this isn't true (*par, birdie, eagle, chip* and *sudden death* are among U.S.-invented golf terms), the expression has been with us at least since the early 1920s and means "a convivial gathering place," like a locker room or bar one goes to after an eighteen-hole round of golf.

**NINTH WAVE.** A superstition among surfers, and previously a nautical superstition of old, holds that waves become progressively higher until the *ninth wave* (some say the tenth), after which the progression begins all over again. While waves sometimes form larger ones when they meet, there is no fixed interval when a large one can be predicted. Nevertheless, surfers all over the world still wait for the legendary *ninth wave.*

**NIP AND TUCK.** *Nip and tuck* pretty much means "neck and neck," but the latter phrase suggests, say, two runners racing at the same speed with neither one ahead of the other, while *nip and tuck* describes a close race where the lead alternates. The earliest recorded form of the expression is found in James K. Paulding's *Westward Ho!* (1832): "There we were at rip and tuck, up one tree and down another." Maybe the *rip* originally came from "let 'er rip" and later became *nip* because of the expression "to nip someone out," to barely beat him, while the *tuck* was simply an old slang word for "vim and vigor." Other guesses at the phrase's origins are even wilder. (*See* NECK AND NECK.)

**NOBLE SCIENCE.** This euphemism for "boxing" dates back to the nineteenth century, when aristocrats like the poet Lord Byron took boxing lessons from pugilists and the ability to box was requisite for a nobleman. Boxing was also dubbed "the manly art of self-defense" at the time.

**NO DICE.** *No dice,* for "no" or "absolutely not," derives from the game of dice, where *no dice* means a throw that doesn't count. *No great shakes,* for "mediocre or rather poor," is also from dice, suggested by the shaking of the dice by players who crap out or otherwise do poorly.

**NO HITS, NO RUNS, NO ERRORS.** Dating back to the 1930s and deriving from its literal use in reports of baseball games, the phrase *no hits, no runs, no errors* has come to mean complete failure, like that of a team shut out with no hits, no runs, no errors. Depending on its use, it can also mean perfection (like the pitcher who pitches a perfect game with no hits, no runs, no errors), and even something uneventful or without hitches (as in a game or inning where there were no hits, no runs, no errors).

**NO HOLDS BARRED.** The expression *no holds barred,* meaning "no limits or reservations, free and uninhibited," was surely suggested by a wrestling contest in which all holds are allowed, but not by an officiated match in which there are rules and regulations. It probably dates back to the nineteenth century.

**NO ROOM TO SWING A CAT.** This phrase may have something to do with the old "sport" of swinging cats by their tails as targets for archers. The words aren't nautical in origin, as is often said. The expression goes back at least to the mid-sixteen hundreds, and *cat-o'-nine-tails* isn't recorded until about 1670, which makes it unlikely that the phrase originated with some sea captain having no room to punish a rebellious sailor with a cat-o'nine tails, or *cat* as it was called for short.

**NOT BY A LONG SHOT.** Whether it was suggested by a difficult shot attempted in archery or shooting isn't known, but the expression *a long shot* first arose in British racing circles some 128 years ago as a bet laid at large odds, a bold wager. *Not by a long shot* therefore means hopelessly out of reckoning. Attempts have been made to derive the saying from the slightly earlier *not by a long chalk,* which comes from the use of chalk for reckoning points in tavern games. But *not by a long chalk* means "not by much," so it seems that the phrase derives from either archery or shooting. (*See* LONG SHOT.)

**NOTHING ON THE BALL.** A baseball pitcher who is pitching poorly (giving up hits) is said to *have nothing on the ball,* the expression dating back to at least 1912, when it is first recorded. Conversely, a pitcher with *something* or *a lot on the ball* is pitching well. The first expression is used generally to describe someone who is incompetent, while the latter means someone who has the ability to succeed. (*See* ON THE BALL.)

**NOT PLAYING WITH A FULL DECK.** *Not playing with a full deck* and its variant, *playing with half a deck,* dates back to the 1960s, when it was first used to mean someone lacking in intelligence; that is, not having the usual allotment of brains. Besides having the obvious connection with a deck of cards, the phrase owes something to the earlier term *not all there,* for "stupid" or "mentally defective," recorded as early as 1821.

**NOT TO GET THE BAT OFF ONE'S SHOULDER.** These words mean not to get a chance, as in, "He had big plans for the company but was fired before he could get the bat off his shoulder." The common expression, first recorded in the 1920s, is obviously from baseball, referring to a batter who takes a strike without even swinging at the ball.

**NOT TO TURN A HAIR.** A horse that *didn't turn a hair* in winning a race on eighteenth-century English race courses was a horse that won a race easily, without working up a sweat or getting its coat ruffled, appearing at the finish line just as it had at the starting line. The phrase was soon used to describe a person who exerts little effort when doing something, who doesn't even *work up a sweat,* a similar expression with the same origin.

**NUDGE.** (*See* GUNCH.)

**NUMBER.** (*See* RETIRING A NUMBER.)

# O

**OFF BASE.** Someone *off base* in today's slang is wrong or badly mistaken. The term refers to a runner in baseball taking a lead so far off the base that he is picked off.

**OFF ONE'S BASE.** To be *off one's base* is to be crazy, mentally unbalanced. Americans have been using this slang term since at least 1912. It has its origins in baseball, suggesting a base runner blithely hanging far off base without any thought of being picked off.

**OFF THE WALL.** Many sports, including handball, squash and racquetball, could be the source of this recent expression meaning "crazy, eccentric, highly unusual, outrageous"—as balls often bounce erratically off walls in all of these games. On the other hand, the term may be related to the earlier expression *bounce off the walls,* referring to the behavior of psychotic patients in mental hospitals.

**OLDER THAN BASEBALL.** An American expression meaning very, very old, as indeed baseball is, especially if one traces it back to the British bat-and-ball game of rounders, which is ancient in origin. *Old* also figures in baseball's most famous song, "Take Me Out to the Ballgame": "For it's one, two, three strikes, you're out, at the old ballgame."

**OLLY, OLLY OXEN FREE.** If you've ever wondered about the origins of this chant—used to call in all players at the end of a game of hide-and-seek—be advised that the experts only have a partial answer to your lifelong puzzlement. Word sleuths are fairly certain that the *oxen* (or *octen*) in the call is simply a childish corruption of "all in."

**ON A SHOESTRING.** *On a shoestring* may come from the card game faro, but it isn't recorded until 1904, although *shoestring gambler* for a "petty tinhorn gambler" is attested to ten years earlier. Meaning to start a business with a small amount of money or capital, *on a shoestring* suggests that one's resources are limited to the shoestring on one's shoes. Living *on a shoestring* means living on a very limited budget.

**ON DECK.** A baseball player batting next in an inning is said to be *on deck,* this obviously an old nautical term put to use on land. So is *in the hole* for the man scheduled to bat third, this a corruption of *in the hold* (below deck)—the reason being that the third batter is *in the hold,* or *hole,* since the second is *on deck.* No one knows who first transferred these nautical words to baseball, but players were using it early in this century.

**ON THE BALL.** Depending on how it is used, this expression has two different origins. *To be on the ball,* "to be alert, knowledgeable, on top of things," probably refers to close and clever following of the ball by players in British soccer or American basketball games. The phrase may have arisen independently in each sport, or it may have originated in the 1940s with "bop and cool" jazz fans, as the *American Dictionary of Slang* suggests. There is no hard evidence for any theory, but the sports analogy seems most logical. To *have something on the ball,* "to be talented or effective in some way," is surely of American origin as a baseball term referring to the various "stuff"—curves, spin, etc.—a good pitcher can put on the ball to frustrate a batter. (*See* NOTHING ON THE BALL.)

**ON THE ROPES.** The allusion here is to a weary, exhausted boxer who is pinned against the ropes in a prizefight and just a punch or two away from being knocked out. The expression dates back long before Mohammed Ali's *rope-a-doping,* in which he used the ropes to his advantage, and figuratively means to be on the edge of ruin. It is first recorded in 1924 but may be much older, for boxing rings have officially had ropes enclosing them since about 1840.

**ON VELVET.** In the game of faro, money won from the house was called *velvet* for some unclear reason and any player who won a lot of money was said to be *on velvet.* From this early-nineteenth-century beginning, *on velvet* passed into general use as a synonym for "an unusual, unexpected profit or gain."

**OPEN AND SHUT.** First recorded in 1848, *open and shut* probably didn't originate in a lawyer's office. A good bet is that it had its origins in some card game, probably either poker or faro. Simpler versions of these games didn't allow complicated betting but shut the pot after it was opened and the ante was put in. The term could have passed into general use from the card tables to take on the meaning of "easily decided or immediately obvious," as in *an open-and-shut* case of murder.

**ORAL DAYS.** When old horse racing buffs talk of the *oral days* they mean the good old days—before the time of totalizer machines—when bets were made by word of mouth. The expression seems to have almost passed out of use, but it is worth remembering.

**OUT IN LEFT FIELD.** Since left field is not any more odd or less active a position than right or center field in baseball, it is hard to understand why it is featured in this common slang expression meaning "very unorthodox and wrong, weirdly unconventional, even crazy." In fact, anyone who has ever played sandlot baseball knows that the most inept (and therefore a little odd, to kids) fielders were relegated to *right* field, because there were fewer left-handed hitters to pull the ball to right field. It has been suggested that the phrase refers to the left field seats in Yankee Stadium that are far away from the coveted seats near Babe Ruth's right field position. Another suggestion links the phrase to the Neuropsychiatric Institute flanking left field in Chicago's nineteenth-century West Side Park, though there are no references to the expression at that time. I would suspect that the words simply refer to the relative remoteness of left field compared to all other positions except center field and that left field is used instead of center field in the expression because *center* by definition means in the middle (of things) and *left* has long had negative associations of clumsiness, awkwardness and radical or eccentric behavior. The expression *from out of left field,* meaning from out of nowhere unexpectedly, lends credence to this remoteness theory. The term *left field* itself was in use by the mid-1860s, along with the names for the other outfield positions, following by twenty years the first recordings of the names for the infield positions.

**OUT OF KILTER.** Many theories have been proposed to explain the origins of *kilter* in this expression, which means to be out of order or out of whack. The best suggestions are *kilter* meaning a "useless hand in cards" from the British dialect term *kilt,* "to make neat," and the Dutch *keelter,* "stomach," because stomachs are often "out of order" with digestive problems. We only know for certain that the expression is first recorded in 1643, as *kelter.*

**OUT OF THE BALLPARK.** (*See* BALLPARK FIGURE.)

**OVERSHOOT THE MARK.** *Overshoot the mark* is an old phrase dating from the late sixteenth century even in its figurative sense of exceeding presented limits, being irrelevant or inappropriate. Its source is probably archery, which was a popular sport for a thousand years in England. (*See* WIDE OF THE MARK.)

# P

**PADDLE BALL.** A fast-growing amateur sport today, *paddle ball* is played with the same basic rules as handball but with short-handled, perforated paddles and a tennis-like ball. The sport was invented in 1930 by University of Michigan physical education teacher Earl Riskey. Riskey even invented the ball and paddle for the game, and along with James Naismith (of basketball fame), William Morgan (the inventor of volleyball), and the Reverend Frank P. Beal (who invented paddle tennis), is one of the four people who are known to have invented a popular sport. (*See* BASKETBALL; HANDBALL; VOLLEYBALL.)

**PADDLE TENNIS.** (*See* PADDLE BALL).

**PALOOKA.** Former baseball player and vaudevillian Jack Conway, who became editor of the show business newspaper *Variety,* is said to have coined the expression *palooka* in about 1920. Walter Winchell called the prolific Conway "my tutor of slanguage"; *belly laugh, pushover, to click* ("succeed"), *baloney* ("bunk"), *S.A.* ("sex appeal"), and *payoff* are among his other memorable coinages. At first a *palooka* meant only a clumsy boxer lacking in ability (despite the comic strip *Joe Palooka*). Then it came to mean any ineffective athlete and finally it was applied to any stupid, clumsy person.

**PAPER CHASE.** Thanks to a 1970s film and television series about the trials of Harvard Law School, *the paper chase* has had currency as a synonym for the hectic, often self-defeating chase after good grades in school as a means for advancement in life. The phrase apparently derives from the ancient game of hares and hounds, also called *the paper chase.* In this game some players (hares) start off in advance on a long run, scattering pieces of paper called "the scent" behind them; the other players (hounds) follow the trail and try to catch the hares before they reach a designated place. (*See* HARRIER.)

**PAR FOR THE COURSE.** *Par* is an American golfing term dating back to 1898 and deriving from the Latin *par,* "equal." It means the score an expert is expected to make on a hole or course, playing in ordinary weather. The expression *par for the course,* meaning just about normal or what one might have expected, owes its life to the golfing term and dates back to about 1920.

**PARLAY.** *Parlay* is an Americanism first recorded in 1828, but probably used before then, that means to wager money on a horse race, cards or other sports event, and continue to bet the original stake plus all winnings on the next race, hand and the like. The word derives from the Italian *parolo,* meaning equal. It has since been extended to mean to use one's money, talent or other assets to achieve a desired objective, such as spectacular wealth or success: "He parlayed his small inheritance into a great fortune."

**PASS THE BUCK.** In American slang, *buck* for "a dollar" may have its origins in animal skins that hunters classified as "bucks" and "does." The buckskins or bucks, larger and more valuable (some five hundred thousand of them were traded each year in eighteenth-century America), could have become a part of American business terminology at the start of the nineteenth century, *buck* later becoming slang for "a dollar." But *buck's* origin could just as well be in poker. A marker called a *buck* was placed next to a poker player in the game's heyday (the mid-nineteenth century) as a reminder that it was that player's turn to deal next. When silver dollars were used as the markers, they could have taken the name *buck* for their own. Although markers called *bucks* may or may not have given us the slang term for a dollar, they are almost certainly responsible for the expression *to pass the buck,* "to evade responsibility"—just as poker players passed on the responsibility for the deal when they passed the marker called the buck. President Harry Truman had a plaque on his desk that read THE BUCK STOPS HERE.

**PAY THROUGH THE NOSE.** Gamblers in the seventeenth century coined the expression *to bleed* a victim. "They will purposely lose some small sum at first, that they may engage him more freely to bleed as they call it," a contemporary writer on card playing noted. He also observed that these same gamblers would "always fix half a score packs of cards" beforehand whenever they intended to bleed a dupe. Once the "coll" had *paid through the nose,* he was "bled white," weak and helpless, until he had "nothing left to lose." The last two expressions arose later but they clearly derive from the gambling term, which was used to describe extortion or blackmail at about the same time. The bloodletting that physicians and barbers commonly used to treat so many diverse illnesses certainly suggested the expression to the gamblers. The bleeding of patients not only made them pale, weak and helpless but often killed them, as it did poet Lord Byron.

**PEA.** (*See* APPLE.)

**PEANUTS, CRACKER JACK.** Vendors have been crying *Peanuts, Cracker Jack!* in ballparks (and at circuses and carnivals) at least since the early 1900s. *Cracker Jack,* now a trademark of the Borden Co., was first sold, under another name, in 1893. The cry is often heard as *Peanuts, popcorn, Cracker Jax* (Jacks)! The words have been inextricably linked with baseball since 1908, when the song "Take Me Out to the Ballgame'' was published, its lyrics including the line ''Buy me some peanuts and crackerjacks; I don't care if I never get back.'' Over 250 million boxes of Crackerjacks are sold every year.

**PELÉ.** This is the nickname of retired Brazilian soccer star Edson Arantes do Nascimento, who is possibly the world's best-known athlete. In his homeland, Pelé, who was born in 1940, is known as the Black Pearl, *Perola Negra* in Portuguese, which is shortened to *Pelé* throughout most of the world. A popular Brazilian coffee is among the several things named after the colorful athlete. And on one occasion a day-long truce was declared in a war between Nigeria and Biafra so that everyone could see *Pelé* play in a scheduled game.

**PHEIDIPPIDES.** (*See* MARATHON.)

**PHENOM.** A *phenom* is short for any exceptionally gifted (or phenomenal) person. The expression first came into use in baseball in the late nineteenth century, when excellent players were called *phenoms.* Soon after it crossed over into general use to mean any gifted person.

**PIGSKIN.** Football players have been calling a football the *pigskin* since at least 1894, when the term was used by Amos Stagg's University of Chicago Maroons, the great football team of that era. At the time all footballs were made of pigskin. (*See* GRAND OLD MAN OF FOOTBALL.)

**PILLAR TO POST.** This expression was first from *post to pillar,* a figure of speech drawn from the old game of court tennis in the fourteenth century or earlier. Court tennis, played indoors, differed in many ways from today's lawn tennis, but even then volleys were crucial to the game. One popular volley was from post to pillar—from a post supporting the net or rope to one of the rear pillars supporting the tennis gallery. Apparently players commonly sustained long volleys between these two points, for by the early fifteenth century Englishmen were regularly using the expression *from post to pillar tossed* outside the game of tennis. In another century the phrase had been reversed to *from pillar to post,* but it still meant the same: "To and fro, hither and thither, from one thing to another without any definite purpose." Modern use of the expression in the sense of going monotonously or fruitlessly from one thing to another is just a logical extension. (*See* LOVE.)

**PINCH HITTER.** An old story has the 1905 New York Giants manager John J. McGraw using one Sammy Strang as baseball's first *pinch hitter* and apparently inventing the term himself. However, this phrase—for a player who bats in a pinch for someone else—had been recorded three years earlier. The expression has wide, general use for any substitute or understudy in any endeavor.

**PING-PONG.** This is a trademark used for table tennis, which was probably derived from the sound of the ball hit during the game. *Ping-pong* also means "to move back and forth rapidly from one thing to another," as in "He was ping-ponged from one doctor to another," this suggested by the rapid volleys in the game.

**PIT BULL.** Dogs of several different breeds—all crosses of bulldogs and terriers—are called *pit bulls.* So is a mongrel-type dog conforming to these general types. All were originally bred for the "sport" of bull-baiting (*see* BULLDOG) and are now used in the cruel blood "sport" of dogfighting. In a small pit or arena, the dogs are paired against each other in a fight to the death while spectators bet on the contest. Such vicious and fearless dogs sporting powerful, tenacious bites have also been used as personal guard dogs in recent times and caused much trouble. One study shows that of twenty-nine dog attack fatalities in the United States over a four-year period, twenty-one were caused by *pit bulls.*

Lately, the term *pit bull* has been extended to mean any very aggressive, mean person who is looking for a fight.

**PITTSBURGH PIRATES.** This baseball team isn't named after any band of pirates that terrorized the seven seas. The team takes its name from the nickname of its first president, J. Palmer "Pirate" O'Neill, who was so-called because he signed a player from another club, pirating him away rather unscrupulously.

**PLAY A HUNCH.** Gamblers once believed that rubbing a hunchback's hump brought good luck. Although the superstition is fortunately all but dead, the expression *to play a hunch,* "to have or act on a lucky notion or premonition," is still frequently heard. The belief that deformed people have special powers or links with the devil is an ancient one, and hunchbacks in particular were believed to share with the devil the ability to see into the future.

**PLAY BALL.** *Play ball* has come to mean to cooperate or collaborate, and also to begin. The words are from baseball, where *Play ball!* has been the plate umpire's command to begin play since at least 1901, when the term first appears in print. *Play ball with* is an extension of the phrase. From the playgrounds where children entreated others to play baseball with them, the expression *play ball with* passed into general use in the 1930s. In one sense it means to cooperate with or to be fair and honest with someone. But more commonly its meaning is to be forced to cooperate with someone in order to receive a favor ("You play ball with me and I'll play ball with you"), or under threat of blackmail or violence ("You play ball with us or else!").

**PLAY BOTH ENDS AGAINST THE MIDDLE.** In faro, America's second favorite game in the nineteenth century (poker was first), *playing both ends against the middle* described the way the dealer provided for a double bet by a player. The phrase came into general use soon after, meaning to use both sides of an argument for your own purpose.

**PLAY-BY-PLAY ACCOUNT.** A detailed, sequential account of any event is called a *play-by-play account* or just a *play-by-play.* The term has been traced back to 1912 in baseball, where it originated; radio *play-by-play* broadcasts of baseball games popularized the phrase.

**PLAY CATCH-UP BALL.** *Play catch-up ball* means to play desperately toward the end of the game when one is losing. Common in the last thirty years or so, the phrase was suggested by the last-minute efforts of college football teams to pull victory from the jaws of defeat, to catch up with their opponents by throwing long, desperate passes (often called "Hail Marys"), etc. The phrase has wide general use, especially when companies approach the end of each fiscal year.

**PLAY CLOSE TO THE VEST.** A cautious cardplayer often holds the cards close to the vest or chest to conceal them from possible cheaters. This old practice suggested the expression *play close to the vest* or *chest,* meaning "to be secretive or uncommunicative about something."

**PLAY FAST AND LOOSE.** This expression for "not being trustworthy or honest, promising one thing and doing another," probably derives from an old con game played by sharpsters at country fairs. In this obsolete game (its exact details long lost), the operator arranged a belt so that a spectator believed he could insert a skewer through its intricate folds and fasten the belt to the table. The spectator would bet that he could do this, but the operator had cleverly coiled the belt so that it only appeared to have a loop in its center and he always pulled it loose from the table after the dupe thought he had skewered it. Metaphorical use of the phrase *to play fast and loose* has been traced back to 1547, so the con game was probably being played before the sixteenth century.

**PLAY FOR FUN.** This term meaning to play for the enjoyment of a game, not for money or with the goal of winning in mind, was originally *to play for love.* It first referred to games of cards played without stakes, the words probably British in origin and dating back to the nineteenth century. (*See* AMATEUR; PLAYING FOR THE LOVE OF IT.)

**PLAY FOR KEEPS.** No one really knows the age of this expression, from the game of marbles. It refers to a marbles game in which players keep the marbles they win; they don't give them back to the loser. In general slang, *to play for keeps* has come to mean to be intent and serious to the point of callousness or to play rough. (*See* PLAY HARDBALL.)

**PLAY HARDBALL.** Baseball was popularly called *hardball* in the early days of the game after the rules were changed so that runners were tagged rather than being hit with the ball to be declared out. This prompted a change from the soft ball formerly used to a hard one and thus the popular name for the game. There was never an official game called *hardball,* but, at least in the 1930s–1960s, the term was common among kids in the Northeast and other areas to distinguish baseball from the game called *softball.* Softball is played with a larger ball (not nearly as hard on the hands for kids catching barehanded) that can't be hit as far; it is also played on a smaller field and the ball is pitched underhanded, among other differences. Perhaps the term *hardball* we now use was born in the sandlots, but that is not certain. In any case, it gave birth in about 1944 to the expression *to play hardball,* which means to act or work aggressively, seriously, competitively or ruthlessly, to play for keeps, not to simply play for fun. Demeaning as it is to softball players, who can be just as serious and competitive as their "hardball" compatriots, the phrase lives on. (*See* PLAY FOR KEEPS.)

**PLAYING FOR THE LOVE OF IT.** There's nothing new about this expression, which means to play a game without stakes for the pleasure of playing. It has its origins in English poet Samuel Butler's very popular satire *Hudibras* (1678), which tells of those who "play for love and money, too." (*See* AMATEUR; LOVE.)

**PLAYING TO THE GRANDSTAND.** *Playing to the grandstand* or *grandstanding* is a baseball term first recorded in 1888 describing a showoff player who tries to make impossible catches or one who makes easy catches appear difficult to the fans in the grandstand. Within a few years such players were called *grandstanders,* and the term was soon applied to a showoff in any endeavor.

**PLAYING WITH LOADED DICE.** Play against someone using loaded dice and you have no chance to win. Dice can be loaded with lead or other weights in such a way that a certain number will always or frequently come up. A gambler can then slip them into a game and throw all sevens, for example, or weight them so that another player will shoot "craps" ("snake-eyes," two ones; or "boxcars," two sixes) on each roll. The practice is as old as the game of dice, but the expression *playing with loaded dice* seems to be a twentieth-century Americanism. It means that someone is cheating or taking unfair advantage.

**PLAYING WITHOUT A FULL DECK.** (*See* NOT PLAYING WITH A FULL DECK.)

**PLAY PENNY POOL.** Anyone who deals in petty, trivial matters can be said to *play penny pool,* like a pool player who gambles for pennies on the outcome of the game or on a shot in the game. The expression is an Americanism dating back fifty years or so.

**PLAY THE FIELD.** In horse racing, *field horses* count as multiple entries and bettors who bet on one of them win if that horse is the winner or if any of the other horses listed with them win the race. This horse racing use of *to play the field* may have suggested the slang term meaning to have a number of lovers, rather than settling (betting) on just one.

**PLIMP.** Back about fifteen years ago *Time* magazine predicted a new verb *to plimp,* meaning "the participatory journalism . . . in which the amateur ventures lamblike among the wolves of professional sport—and then writes about how to be a lamb chop." Said verb is based on the name of American author George A. Plimpton, who has written a number of books about his adventures playing with professionals in various sports. The eponymous word isn't yet included in any major dictionary, but it has entered the language, having been noted in several books besides this one.

**PLUG-UGLY.** *Plug-ugly* is an old term for a prizefighter that was first used in 1856 to describe a city ruffian, rowdy or any such disreputable character. One theory says fighters were so named because such persons are ugly from being plugged (punched) in the face. Another source claims the expression "derived in Baltimore . . . from a short spike fastened in the toes of [gang members'] boots, with which they kicked their opponents in a dense crowd, or as they elegantly expressed it, 'plugged them ugly.' "

**POES OF PRINCETON.** Edgar Allan Poe is arguably America's best-known poet. Few are aware, however, that he was an excellent athlete as well. Poe, who would hardly suggest anything but an emaciated aesthete to anyone today, long-jumped twenty-one feet while at West Point. He was as good a swimmer as Lord Byron (who swam the Hellespont), and once swam seven and a half miles from Richmond to Warwick, Virginia, "against a tide running two to three miles an hour." Another time he boxed the ears of and horse-whipped a scurrilous critic. He is also remembered for the *Poes of Princeton,* football players famous in their time if now all but forgotten. They were six members of the 1899 Princeton college football team, each named Poe and each a great-nephew of the poet. All of them apparently inherited Uncle Edgar's athletic prowess, but none his poetic genius off the field.

**POINT-BLANK.** A *point-blank* shot made by archers in sixteenth-century England was one in which the arrow was aimed or pointed directly at the small white, or blank, bull's-eye in the center of the target. With the advent of firearms, a shot was said to be *point-blank* when it remained approximately straight over a certain distance. Because close-range, *point-blank* firing in gunnery led to immediate destruction, the term became a synonym for direct, uncompromising rejection or blunt, brutal frankness in such terms as *point-blank refusal* and *point-blank denial.* (*See* BULL'S-EYE.)

**POKER.** *Poker* takes its name from the French *poque* for a similar card game, although the rules of the Persian game *As Nas* (played with five cards) and *poque* (played with three cards) were combined to create America's characteristic gambling game. The game is mentioned as early as 1834 and probably dates back even further.

Good poker players never reveal the contents of their hands with a joyous or a disappointed expression. The American term *poker face* for their deadpan expression has been around as long as the game and has been used for almost as long in different contexts.

**POLO.** One of the relatively few Tibetan words in English, *polo* derives from the Tibetan *pulu,* for the name of the ball hit with the mallet in this game played on horseback. Polo probably originated in Tibet, was adopted by the Indians, and borrowed from them by British soldiers serving in India during the mid–eighteenth century. Other English words whose ultimate ancestry is Tibetan include "panda" and "yak."

**PRO.** One dictionary says the short form *pro* for a *professional* is first recorded in about 1850, so it could have originated in baseball, though there is no proof of this nor of any other origin. The first recorded mention of *professional* players in baseball is in 1867, when the Rockford, Illinois, team began paying salaries to expert players prompting amateur "gentlemen players" all over to complain about the practice. But by 1869 baseball's first professional team, the Cincinnati Red Stockings, was touring the country and a new age in the sport had begun. (*See* AMATEUR.)

**PRO BOWL.** (*See* ALL-STAR.)

**PULL A BRODIE.** (*See* DO A BRODIE.)

**PULL A FAST ONE.** *Pull* has been slang for "to engineer a deception" for well over a century, but the expression *to pull a fast one,* "to put over a trick or clever swindle," goes back to only about 1938. Baseball seems the obvious source—a pitcher coming in hard with a fast ball after throwing a lot of "junk." But the nod has to go to "fast-bowling at cricket," however, as the expression is first recorded in England. (*See* CRICKET.)

**PULL THE STRING.** To *pull the string* is to pitch a change-of-pace ball to a baseball batter to put him off-balance. The pitcher usually throws a fast ball first; his next pitch is a slow ball which to the off-balance batter appears to be "attached to and pulled back by a string." Quoting Burt Dunne's pamphlet collection *The Folger Dictionary of Baseball* (1958) in his *The Dickson Baseball Dictionary,* Paul Dickson tells a good story about another possible, if unlikely derivation: "Burt Dunne says this is derived from a trick featuring 'a trapped badger' in a box overhead. The rookie releases the 'badger' by pulling the string, and says Dunne, 'down come refuse—and worse.' "

**PUMPING IRON.** This term, meaning "lifting weights," became popular in the 1970s, largely because of body-builder Arnold Schwarzenegger's efforts to promote the health benefits of weight lifting.

**PUNCH-DRUNK.** Some boxers have suffered brain damage from repeated blows to the head. The most common symptoms of this injury are poor coordination, slurred speech, mental deterioration and a broad-based gait. Old, very impaired fighters suffering from this combination of effects were given the name *punch-drunk* by Dr. Harrison S. Martland in a 1928 article in the *Journal of the American Medical Association.* However, Dr. Martland probably did not coin the term, as *punch-drunk* is recorded in America as early as 1915. In the early 1940s *punchy* began to supplant *punch-drunk.*

**PUNCHING BAG.** Someone who takes much abuse and punishment is said to be a *punching bag.* The term is American and comes from boxing; it is first recorded in 1897, although boxers practiced on heavy bags filled with sand long before then.

**PUNTER.** A *punter* has been slang for "a gambler or a bettor" since the early eighteenth century. This word has its origins in the French *punter,* meaning to place a bet against the bank in the game of faro. The football *punter,* or kicker, is of different yet uncertain ancestry, perhaps being of echoic origin from the sound of the ball when kicked.

**PUT IN ONE'S BEST LICKS.** (*See* LAST LICKS.)

**PUT ON THE GLOVES.** Since about 1847, to *put on the gloves* has meant to fight, in a ring or elsewhere, although boxing gloves only became mandatory under the Queensberry rules. Boxing gloves were used in England as early as 1734 but weren't commonly called by that name until about 1875; prior to that, they were called *mufflers, gloves* and *padded mittens.* (*See* BELOW THE BELT.)

**PUTT.** According to most sports historians, *putt* is simply a Scottish pronunciation and spelling of *put,* which was first recorded in 1743. Thus to *putt* a golf ball into the hole is to put it in the hole. Those who trace the origin of golf to Holland, however, believe that *putt* derives from the Dutch word for the hole itself.

**PUT UP YOUR DUKES.** *Dukes,* for "fists," probably honors the duke of York, Frederick Augustus (1763–1820), the second son of England's George III. A total loss as commander in chief of the army, Frederick was nevertheless popular among his subjects. As he had once duelled in public with the future duke of Richmond, his name was associated with fighting, and being an ardent sportsman, he was often seen at the racetrack and prizefighting ring. Possibly this led boxers to nickname their fists *dukes of York,* and the phrase was shortened to *dukes,* from which came the common expression *put up your dukes,* "let's fight." Or else, *duke of Yorks,* Cockney rhyming slang for "forks," was associated with fingers, then hands and finally fists, or *dukes*—with the duke of York somewhere in mind. Another more ingenious explanation has it that noses were called *dukes* because the duke of Wellington's nose was big—fists therefore being dubbed *duke busters,* which ultimately became *dukes.* The duke may have been immortalized in the language, but he ended his career in disgrace when his mistress admitted to taking bribes with his permission. To save face, he had to pay her off so that she wouldn't publish his love letters.

# Q

**QUARRY.** The *quarry* is now the object of any chase—the deer in hunting, the bird attacked in falconry—but it once meant something entirely different. In the Middle Ages, the *quarry* (the word deriving from the Latin *corium,* "skin") was the entrails of the deer given to the hounds after a hunt as a reward. (The *quarry* in *stone quarry* has a different origin, from the Latin *quadraia,* "the place where stone is squared," or cut into blocks.)

**QUARTERBACK.** Football's *quarterback,* the backfield player who directs the offensive play of a team on the field, suggested this general verb meaning "to lead, direct or manage anything." The term has been in use for a good fifty years. (*See* MONDAY MORNING QUARTERBACK.)

**QUARTER HORSE.** *Quarter horses* are named for their ability to run well in quarter-mile races, not because of their size or lineage. The term is an Americanism first recorded in 1834, though *quarter races* are mentioned a good fifty years earlier as being very popular in the South. Quarter horses, usually smaller than thoroughbred racehorses, were also called *quarter nags.*

**QUEEN CAMILLA.** (*See* FAST AS LADAS.)

**QUEENSBERRY RULES.** (*See* BELOW THE BELT.)

**QUICK AS YOU CAN SAY JACK ROBINSON.** (*See* JACK ROBINSON.)

# R

**RACE IS NOT TO THE SWIFT.** "The race is not to the swift, nor the battle to the strong," according to Ecclesiastes 9:11. The biblical phrase has become proverbial over the past four hundred years and has several humorous variations, including American humorist Franklin Pierce Adams's much quoted "The race is not the swift, nor the battle to the strong; but the betting is best that way."

**RACKET.** In tennis and similar games, the ball was originally hit with the palm of the hand, which was called *raquette* in Old French, deriving ultimately from the Arabic *rahat* meaning the same. In the evolution of tennis, various gloves were used next, then boards, then a short paddle and finally the long-handled instrument employed today. All were called by the name *raquette,* which became the English word *racket.* The French still call tennis *le jeu de paume,* the palm game. Incidentally, the tennis word *racket* has no etymological connection with the old onomatopoeic English word *racket* for noise, which is probably responsible in a roundabout way for the *racket* meaning a criminal activity.

**RAIN CHECK.** An old story says the rain check—the detachable part of a ticket that a spectator uses to gain admission to a future game if the current game is postponed because of rain—was invented by Abner Powell of the minor league New Orleans Pelicans in 1888. Powell conceived the idea, according to the tale, because when his club's games were rained out, people who hadn't attended the rain out lined up to get replacement tickets for the next game, costing him a lot of money. The story sounds good, but the term *rain check* is first recorded four years earlier in St. Louis. Rain checks aren't common these days, as tickets usually list the rain date. The term is widely used today to mean an offered or requested postponement of an invitation until another time.

**READ 'EM AND WEEP.** A common cry of a cardplayer or crap shooter after a good hand or roll of the dice. The American expression is now used generally to mean "here's some very unwelcome information for you, information that will benefit me."

**REAL McCOY.** Kid McCoy happened to hear a barroom braggart claim that he could lick any of the McCoys around—any time, any place. The Kid, then at the top of his boxing division, promptly delivered his Sunday punch in person. When the challenger came to, he qualified his statement by saying that he had only meant that he could beat any of the other fighters around who were using the Kid's name, not *the real McCoy* himself. In another version of the story, which also takes place in a saloon, a heckler sneers that if the Kid was *the real McCoy,* he'd put up his dukes and prove it. McCoy does so and the heckler, rubbing his jaw from his seat in the sawdust, exclaims, "That's the real McCoy, all right."

But there have been numerous, unproved explanations for the origin of *the real McCoy* for "the genuine, the real thing." Still another is that advertisements of Kid McCoy's fights proclaimed that *the real McCoy,* and not some imitation, would appear. The fabulous Kid McCoy won the welterweight title in 1896, but outgrew his class; he was once ranked by *Ring Magazine* as the greatest light heavyweight of all time, though he never held this title. It is possible that the use of his name may have been strengthened by the ring exploits of Al McCoy, who held the middleweight title from 1919 to 1917. Certainly there were a lot of McCoys around in the early days of boxing, among the myriad Mysterious Billy Smiths, Dixie Kids, Honey Melodys and Philadelphia Jack O'Briens. But which McCoy is *the real McCoy* remains open to debate; he may not even have been a boxer. (*See* PUT UP YOUR DUKES.)

**REBOUND.** (*See* CATCH ON THE REBOUND.)

**RED DOG.** Linebackers "hound" or "dog" the passer in a football *red dog,* crashing through the line to try to break up a play. When the tactic was invented in the 1960s, "red dog" was the signal given in the huddle if one linebacker was to try cracking the line, "blue dog" if two were to be used, and "green dog" if all three linebackers were to charge. Football fans, however, misused the terms and applied *red dog* to any rush through the offensive line, made by linebackers or linemen, and that is what the term means today. It has also been used outside of football for a rush on one person by a group of youths, usually drunk or demented.

**REGATTA.** Back in the seventeenth century, a *regatta* was a race between gondolas on the Grand Canal in Venice. This Venetian dialect word translates as "a strife or contention or struggling for mastery." The first English *regatta,* or yacht race, was held on the River Thames on June 23, 1775. The word is still used to describe any series of boat races.

**RELAY.** Today's track *relay* races have their etymological origin in hunting, where packs of fresh hounds were held at strategic points along a hunting route so that they could relieve the hounds that tired. In fact, the word *relay* derives ultimately from the obsolete French verb *relayer,* meaning "to loose the hounds."

**RETIRING A NUMBER.** Track competitors were the first athletes to wear numbers identifying them. Washington and Jefferson University had the first football team to do so, in 1908, and the 1929 New York Yankees were the first baseball team to adopt the practice (their numbers originally noted the player's place in the batting order). Soon the numbers of great players were retired when they retired from a sport, this being among the greatest honors a player could receive. The first player to have a number retired in any sport seems to have been football's Harold "Red" Grange, when he was at the University of Illinois. Grange, also known as "77" and most famously as the Galloping Ghost, later became a professional football star and a television sportscaster. Sportswriter Grantland Rice coined "Galloping Ghost" on the same weekend (October 18–19, 1920) that he coined the memorable "Four Horsemen." (*See* FOUR HORSEMEN.)

**RHUBARB.** Speculation has been rife for years about how the slang term *rhubarb,* "a heated argument," arose from the name of a popular vegetable. Since the word is often associated with baseball, many writers say it has its origins there. But probably the best explanation, advanced about twenty-five years ago by a veteran actor familiar with theatrical traditions, is that actors simulating angry talk in crowd scenes for "the noise without" gathered backstage and "intoned the sonorous word 'rhubarb.' " This theatrical tradition possibly goes back to Shakespearean times, but the slang *rhubarb* for an argument arose only in the late nineteenth century. It therefore came to mean a "rumpus" or a "row" at about the time baseball was fast becoming America's national pastime. It is easy to see how the stage term could have been applied to an argument on the diamond, especially a mass argument that involved both teams, although there is no solid proof of this. Fortunately for the vegetable's reputation, baseball's *rhubarbs* don't result from the ingestion of the plant. *Rhubarb* itself has an interesting derivation, taking its name from the Latin *rhabarbarum.* The Romans called it this because the plant was native to the river Rha (the Volga), a foreign "barbarian" territory—*rha barbaron,* the plant's name, thus meaning "from the barbarian (foreign) Rha." The first *rhubarb* planted in America was sent to the great naturalist John Bartram from Siberia in 1770.

**RIGHT BOWER.** *Right bower* used to be more frequently employed for someone's "right-hand man," like Sherlock Holmes's Dr. Watson. The expression is from the card game euchre, seldom played anymore, in which the right bower is the jack of trumps, among the most powerful cards in the deck.

**RIGHT OFF THE BAT.** The sound of a baseball hit sharply on the meat of a bat inspired the Americanism *right off the bat,* meaning at once, immediately, very quickly, the first thing. It is first recorded in 1910.

**RIGHT UP MY ALLEY.** An inside-the-park home run in baseball is often hit *right down the alley,* between two fielders, but I doubt that this is the source of the above phrase, which is sometimes *right down my alley.* The expression, meaning "very familiar and appealing to me," probably has nothing to do with a bowling alley, either. *My alley* here seems to be a synonym for my street, the place where I live and where I'm most at home.

**RINGER.** A *ringer* is a counterfeit, especially a superior horse passed off as an unknown, or a professional athlete posing as an amateur. The word may derive, as *Webster's* says, from the old bell ringer's expression *ring in,* working a certain bell into a performance. But there seems to be very little evidence linking bell ringers with horse racing, sports and gamblers. Perhaps a better explanation is that *ringer* was once a slang term for "counterfeit," which derives from the sale of brass rings for gold at country fairs. *Dead ringer* has no sinister connotations. It simply means a perfect imitation of something or a person with an uncanny resemblance to someone else. It derives from *ringer,* with *dead* in this case meaning "absolute" or "complete." For a fabled example of a *ringer* see the entry for *dark horse.*

**ROLL WITH THE PUNCHES.** An expression from the boxing arena that probably dates to the nineteenth century, *to roll with the punches* is based on the way a good, experienced boxer takes a punch. It means, of course, to take the blows of fate as they come, bending with them but springing back and moving on.

**ROOKIE.** There is much dispute about *rookie's* origin. Some authorities trace the word to a shortening of *recruit,* a term first used in baseball at the end of the nineteenth century, and others suggest the rook from the game of chess as the source. Most etymologists, however, agree with Eric Partridge who claims *rookie* as British army slang for a raw recruit as well as a pun on *rooky,* British slang for a rascally person. It is possible, if not probable, that *rookie* had an independent coinage from *recruit* in American baseball and it is certain that the word achieved its popularity in the United States from its common use in baseball for "a player playing his first season in the Major Leagues." Now *rookie* can refer to a first-year player in any sport, as well an army recruit, or any neophyte.

**ROPE-A-DOPE.** (*See* ON THE ROPES.)

**ROUNDHEELS.** *Roundheels* has been slang for a prostitute or a promiscuous woman since at least the early 1940s. The expression derives from the 1920s boxing term *roundheels* for an inferior boxer who is more often on his back than his feet.

**RUBBER MATCH.** A *rubber match* or *rubber game* or simply *rubber* in any sport means a deciding contest between two tied opponents. The term dates back to the late sixteenth century but no one seems certain of its etymology or in what sport it originated. The expression was not used in card games until the mid-eighteenth century and the earliest recorded use of it appears to be a 1599 reference, cited in the *Oxford English Dictionary,* to the game of bowls. The word *rubber* in the term seems to derive from a word of unknown origin, not the resilient substance called "rubber" or the verb "to rub."

**RUGBY.** In 1823 at a football game at the *Rugby School* in England, a young player named William Ellis picked up the ball and ran down field with it, an unsportsmanlike maneuver at the time for which Ellis profusely apologized. But his play caught on and began to be imitated by other players, which of course inspired the defense to stop the ball carriers by tackling them, another practice unthinkable under the old rules of the game. This type of football began to be called *rugby football* or simply *rugby* and another rule of the new game allowed a player to run with the ball if it was caught on the fly or on the first bounce. Players who preferred the old, no-ball-carrying football formed the London Football Association in 1863 and published their own rules. Their brand of football was called *association football,* which became *assoc football. Assoc football* was shortened to *soc,* to which an *er* ending was added, giving us the word *soccer* for the game. (*See* FOOTBALL.)

**RUN FOR YOUR LIFE.** According to one old tale, a fast runner of the duke of Monmouth was captured during the battle of Sedgemoor in 1685 and told that he could *run for his life,* that is, his life would be spared if he could outrun a horse. The contest was held, the horse lost the long race, and the runner was freed. This is supposed to be the origin of *to run for your life,* though it was probably common long before any such race—if indeed there was one. It is, however, possible for a good runner to beat a horse in a long race like a marathon.

**RUN RIOT.** *The Master of Game,* a hunting manual published in 1410, explains that to *run riot* was originally a term describing a hunting dog who, after losing the scent of the animal he was chasing, began acting unruly and undisciplined, often running after other animals instead of the intended quarry. Over the next century the phrase came into its current usage for anyone acting without constraint or control.

**RUSSIAN ROULETTE.** Sad to say, *Russian roulette* is played as a game throughout the world, as harrowing scenes in the movie *The Deerhunter* reveal. It is, to say the least, a game of high risk in which each player spins the cylinder of a revolver containing one bullet, points the muzzle at the temple and pulls the trigger. The *roulette* in the phrase is from the gambling game of *roulette,* which is French for "little wheel." The *Russian* may be there because czarist Russian officers played the game, but there is no solid evidence of this and the term is not recorded before 1935.

# S

**SAFARI.** *Safaris* are getting back to the original meaning of the word. Once exclusively hunting trips into the African jungle, they are now often sightseeing excursions for camera-toting tourists, more in keeping with the Arabic root word *safara,* "travel."

**SANDLOT BASEBALL.** Since the early twentieth century, *sandlot baseball* has meant unorganized baseball games played by youngsters or loosely organized leagues of semiprofessional players. The term *sandlot* was made popular in 1880 by San Francisco's Sand-lot Party of workingmen, who held their meetings in vacant sand lots. *Sandlot* is also used as a synonym for anything amateur, though not so often as *bush league* or *bush.*

**SATCHEL PAIGE'S RULES.** (*See* DON'T LOOK BACK, SOMETHING MIGHT BE GAINING ON YOU.)

**SAVED BY THE BELL.** An expression first used in boxing, *saved by the bell* means to be rescued from something at the last moment. It originally described a fighter about to be counted out when the bell ending the round rings, saving him at least for another round. This practice became mandatory under the Queensberry rules, introduced in 1867.

**SAY IT AIN'T SO, JOE.** They said Shoeless Joe Jackson was so poor he played ball without shoes down home in South

Carolina, but he put on spikes when he made the Majors and became a great star. His lifetime average of .356 is the third highest in the history of baseball. Shoeless Joe never made Cooperstown's Hall of Fame, though, and probably never will. Jackson was one of the eight Chicago White Sox players who was indicted for conspiring with gamblers to throw the 1919 World Series, after which he was banished from baseball for life. After being indicted for his role in the affair on September 28, 1920, Jackson walked down the steps of the Cook County courthouse through a crowd of reporters and a ragged little boy grabbed his sleeve and said "Say it ain't so, Joe." The phrase is still used in reference to any hero who has betrayed his trust, although there is some question about Jackson's guilt (after all, he batted .375 in the Series and made no fielding errors) and he was later acquitted by Judge Landis. (*See* BLACK BETSY.)

**SCHNEIDER.** It seems the only Schneider whose name definitely became a word is the German C. V. Schneider (1610–1680). As a result of his anatomical research, the *Schneiderian membrane,* or mucous membrane of the nose, is named after him. But there may be a case for the gin rummy *schneider:* One *schneiders* or *schneids* an opponent in gin rummy by winning before the opponent has scored a single point. Did some gin champion named Schneider do this so often that the feat came to be named after him? Or does the word derive from the German *Schneider* for "tailor," as most scholars believe? The term is apparently an Americanism, in use only since 1940. Perhaps it comes from "tailor" because tailors cut clothes down and *schneiders* cut down the size of the loser's bankroll!

**SCORE.** The earliest counting was recorded by making notches on sticks, and the earliest scores of games may have been recorded in this way, too. But though our word *score* derives from the Old Norse *skor,* meaning "notch," the use of *score* for a record of points won in games is a relatively recent development, only dating back to the nineteenth century, when it was popularized by English game authority Edmund Hoyle. (*See* ACCORDING TO HOYLE.)

**SCREWBALL.** "King Carl" Hubbell is probably responsible for this thirties' expression meaning an eccentric person. The New York Giants pitcher used his famous *screwball,* which he introduced in the early 1930s, to win twenty-four games in a row. Hubbell pitched forty-six consecutive scoreless innings and, most amazing of all, struck out in order the greatest concentration of slugging power ever assembled—Babe Ruth, Lou Gehrig and Jimmy Foxx—in the 1934 all-star game.

**SCRIMMAGE.** The football term *scrimmage* for the action that takes place between two teams from the moment the ball is snapped until it is declared dead is related to the military *skirmish,* for a brief fight. *Scrimmage* is a variation of the latter word, which originally referred to a medieval sword fight. A *scrimmage* can also be a practice game played by two teams.

**SCRUB TEAM.** Dating back to at least the sixteenth century, the English word *scrub* meant "small stunted trees or cattle." In America, by the early nineteenth century, *scrub* commonly meant "inferior" as well as "dwarf." By the end of the century it was being applied to second-rate college football teams, these *scrub teams* also called "second teams." The term *scrub team* therefore has nothing at all to do with how often the team members bathed, as *scrub* for "to wash vigorously" derives from the Middle English *scrubbe* meaning the same.

**SCUBA.** *Scuba* is simply an acronym standing for "*s*elf-*c*ontained *u*nderwater *b*reathing *a*pparatus." Popular since World War II, *scuba diving* has enabled millions to see underwater sights previously the province of a few thousand professional divers. (*See* SNORKELING.)

**SEEING STARS.** The expression *seeing stars* is frequently used to describe fighters hit hard on the head. There is a 1609 quotation that seems to imply its use, but it is first recorded in the 1891 *Century Dictionary*: "*To see stars*, to have a sensation as of flashes of light, produced by a sudden jarring of the head, as by a direct blow." The phenomenon results from a change in blood flow to the brain. According to neurologist Dr. C. Boyd Campbell: "Blood supplies nerve cells with oxygen, sugar, and other vital nutrients. Any loss of blood to the brain—easily caused by standing up, an action that forces blood away from the head—deprives the nerve cells of these nutrients. This causes a brief, random firing of neurons, which is interpreted by the brain's visual cortex as quick flashes of light, or 'stars.' The phenomenon is also produced by a blow to the head or by stimulating the eye electrically, both of which alter the normal state of nerve cells."

**SEND TO THE SHOWERS.** This phrase, meaning "to dismiss or reject someone," is from baseball, where it is first recorded in 1931. In baseball it means to take a failing pitcher out of a game and send in a relief pitcher. Since the pitcher can't play again in that game, he often takes a shower in the clubhouse and changes to street clothes.

**SEVENTH-INNING STRETCH.** These words have become synonymous for a brief break from any long period of sitting. They come from baseball's traditional *seventh-inning stretch,* which dates back to the late nineteenth century. One theory credits the ritual to President William Howard Taft, who is said to have stood up to stretch in the seventh inning of a Washington Senators game, prompting the rest of the crowd to follow suit. Better documented is the theory that the tradition originated at a 1882 game at Manhattan

College in New York City. Manhattan College baseball coach Brother Jasper, also the prefect of discipline, instructed restless students in the stands to rise and stretch for a minute in the seventh inning before the game continued. This *seventh-inning stretch* became a ritual at all Manhattan College games and spread to the Major Leagues during the 1880s when the college team played exhibition games against the New York Giants in the Polo Grounds.

**SHELL GAME.** (*See* THIMBLERIG.)

**SHOOT ONE'S BOLT.** The *bolt* in the phrase *he's shot his bolt,* meaning he's finished with his efforts, is not a door bolt, but an arrow—a bolt in archery being an arrow with a bulletlike knob. Among other words and phrases owing their origin to the arrow of archery are *thunderbolt, a bolt from the blue,* "a complete surprise" and *to bolt upright.*

**SHOW THE WHITE FEATHER.** A cock with any white feathers was believed to be poorly bred and too cowardly for cockfighting in days past. This led to the old expression *to show the white feather,* "to exhibit cowardice."

**SHUT OUT.** Though the term is most commonly heard in baseball for a game in which the losing team doesn't score, *shut out* probably has its origins in horse racing. First recorded in 1855, *shut out* has long referred to a bettor who arrives at a track window when it is too late to bet, thus being *shut out* by the closed window. Today someone who fails to make any headway in any endeavor is said to be *shut out.*

**SIXES AND SEVENS.** I'm at *sixes and sevens*—in a state of confusion—trying to explain this expression, which dates back to about 1340. One theory is that it comes from the biblical phrase (Job 5:19): "He shall deliver thee in six troubles: yea in seven there shall be no evil touch thee."

More likely the term evolved from the ancient dice game of hazard. *Sinque* and *sice* (''five'' and ''six'') were the most risky bets to make in the old game, and anyone who tried to throw these numbers was considered careless and confused. Later, *sinque* and *sice* became ''six'' and ''seven.'' Perhaps the change simply occurred because the terms looked and sounded somewhat alike. Only about a century and a half ago did *set at six and seven* take on its plural form and become *at sixes and sevens.* The phrase is still widely used today.

**SKATE ON THIN ICE.** The allusion here is to skating over ice so thin that it hardly bears the skater's weight. This was actually once a sport called *tidkledybendo* in New England. The metaphor *skating on thin ice* means that someone is taking chances, or behaving in a questionable, dangerous or indelicate manner.

**SLAM DUNK.** *Dunk* simply meant to shoot a basketball through the goal in the 1930s when the term is first recorded. But in the mid-1960s tall players developed what is known as the *dunk shot* by leaping above the basket and stuffing the ball in. The *slam dunk* came soon after, this a more theatrical version of the dunk shot in which the ball is slammed down through the hoop.

**SLAP-HAPPY.** The internal rhyme of this word has insured its long life, which dates back at least to the late 1920s. It means to be very confused, dazed or punch-drunk, and comes from the sport of boxing, which has produced too many men who act like this because of too many blows landed on the head. Despite his nickname, clowning boxer Slapsy Maxie Rosenbloom was *not* one of them. (*See* PUNCH-DRUNK.)

**SLEEPER.** A *sleeper* can be anything from a movie or book that unexpectedly achieves great success, to a cunning football player who unexpectedly gets the ball and runs. In either case, it probably derives from the mid–nineteenth-century gambling term *sleeper* that was used to mean "an unexpected winning card."

**SLIDE, KELLY, SLIDE.** As Dizzy Dean would have put it, when Kelly "slud," he slud hard. Michael Joseph "King" Kelly, who played ball for Chicago and Boston in the 1880s, was a talented hustling player called the Ten Thousand Dollar Beauty because he signed for that then incredible sum one year. In 1889 a song was written about Kelly by his friend, monologuist John W. Kelly, exhorting him to *slide, Kelly, slide,* an expression which has become proverbial. Kelly innovated a number of techniques beside the "hook" or "fadeaway" slide. As a catcher he invented the dirty trick of throwing his mask up the first-base line in order to trip a batter trying to beat out a hit. Kelly played to win. As Boston's manager, he looked up from the bench one day to see a foul ball drifting toward him. At the time, baseball rules specified that substitutions could be made at any point in the game, and seeing that the Boston catcher could not possibly reach the foul, Kelly jumped up off the bench, shouted "Kelly now catching for Boston," and caught the ball for an out. His maneuver led to the rule now on the books that substitutions can only be made when the ball isn't in play.

**SLOW AND STEADY WINS THE RACE.** When Charles Darwin measured the speed of a Galapagos turtle by walking beside it, he found that it "walked at the rate of sixty yards in ten minutes, that is 360 yards in an hour, or four miles a day—allowing a little time for it to eat on the road." That is certainly slow enough for an expression *slow as a tortoise,* but the creature, unlike the snail, has been noted for his reliability rather than his lack of speed. The expression *slow and steady wins the race* is from the poem "The Hare and the Tortoise" by Robert Lloyd (1733–1764) but can be traced back to Aesop's fable "The Hare and the Tortoise," in which the hare awakens to see the tortoise crossing the finish line in a race the hare was sure he would win.

**SLUGGER.** The term *to slug,* "to hit hard," has been used in baseball since the 1860s and *slugger* for a hard or heavy hitter is recorded as early as 1883. But *slugger* was used in reference to a hard-hitting boxer before this, as well as to a cricket batter. Possibly the word derives from the early expression *to hit with a slug,* that is, a piece of heavy metal-like lead fired from a gun.

**SMILEY.** *Smiley,* or *smilie,* is an unusual word for a cut made by a club on the face of a golf ball, which somewhat resembles a smile. The term only dates back to the 1970s. (*See* DIMPLES.)

**SNAKE EYES.** (*See* WITHIN AN ACE OF.)

**SNEAKERS.** The first *sneakers* were made in 1868 but the athletic shoes weren't called *sneakers* until about 1895. Once worn in many sports, the fabric and rubber shoes may have been so named because baseball players "stealing" bases favored them, or because thieves found them useful in their line of work. The word is an Americanism made, of course, from the word *sneak.* The British call these shoes *plimsols,* after Samuel Plimsol, who in 1875 invented the *Plimsol marks* on cargo ship hulls that indicated the depth to which these ships may be safely loaded—because the shoes were often worn by sailors and have a mudguard that resembles a *Plimsol mark.*

**SNIPER.** The snipe is a wary, quick bird that wealthy hunters had no success with in England until the bow and arrow was replaced with the gun in the sixteenth century. Even then the bird was difficult to bag unless the hunter concealed himself and patiently waited for a good shot. Snipe shooting became a favorite sport because of its difficulty; because of the snipe-hunter's *modus operandi, sniper* came to mean any marksman firing from a concealed position.

**SNORKELING.** The *snorkel,* introduced during World War II, was at first only a retractable tube that ventilated a sub cruising slightly below the surface. It took its name from the German *schnorchel,* "air intake." After the war, *snorkel* became better known as a tube to breathe through while swimming face down in the water or slightly below the surface, this new sport called *snorkeling.* (*See* SCUBA.)

**SOCCER.** (*See* RUGBY.)

**SOFTBALL.** (*See* PLAY HARDBALL.)

**SOLAR PLEXUS.** This term was first used as a synonym for the pit of the stomach in the 1890s by American fighters. Before this it had meant the network of nerves behind the stomach. Gentleman Jim Corbett lost the heavyweight championship in 1897 when Bob "Fitz" Fitzsimmons knocked him out with a blow to the *solar plexus.*

**SOLITAIRE.** (*See* CANFIELD.)

**SOMETHING ON THE BALL.** A baseball pitcher with *something on the ball* has the ability to throw a variety of pitches that are usually effective. Since the early 1900s the phrase has been extended to mean anyone with skill or ability. (*See* NOTHING ON THE BALL; ON THE BALL.)

**SOUTHPAW.** Humorist Finley Peter Dunne, then a sportswriter, is usually said to have coined this word for a left-handed baseball pitcher while covering sports for the *Chicago Herald* in 1891. Home plate in the old Chicago ballpark was then to the west, so that a left-handed pitcher released the ball from the "paw," or hand, on this south side. The word soon came to describe any left-hander. While there are major doubts that Dunne invented the phrase—for one thing it is first recorded six years earlier—it is probable that *southpaw* was invented for the same reason cited in the above story.

**SPALDING.** Alfred Goodwill *Spalding* (1850–1915) deserves his place in baseball's Hall of Fame as much as any man. He may not be the Father of Baseball, but he is certainly a Father of *the* Baseball. It was only when he came on the scene with his precise manufacturing methods that what had been a chaotic minor sport was fashioned into the national pastime. Lively balls were once so rubbery that baseball scores like 201–11 were not uncommon, and others so dead that the phrase "fell with a dull thud" found its way into the language. The former Chicago White Sox manager did not invent the hard ball when he founded his company in 1880, but the rigid manufacturing standards he maintained made it possible for the newly formed National League of Professional Baseball to survive. Such careful preparations over the years have made the *Spalding* trademark synonymous for a baseball. Other sporting equipment manufactured by the firm includes a pink rubber ball called the *Spalding*, which has been commonly known to several generations of American youngsters as the "spaldeen."

**SPIN DOCTOR.** A *spin doctor* is an advisor of a politician who interprets or slants stories to the media in his client's favor. *Spin* here is probably from the spin a pitcher puts on a baseball to make it curve; thus the *spin doctor* is throwing the media a curve. The term is a new one only frequently heard in the last few years. (*See* THROW SOMEONE A CURVE.)

**SPINNAKER.** The most probable explanation we have for this word is that back in the 1860s an unknown yacht owner invented a sail rigged at right angles from his racing vessel's side, a sail that extended from masthead to deck and ballooned far out to take advantage of the slightest breeze. The racing vessel was named *Sphinx,* but its crew had difficulty pronouncing its name, calling it *Spinnicks.* Thus, the new sail was referred to as *Spinnicker's sail* and finally became known as a *spinnaker.*

**SPITBALL.** *Spitball* is now used outside of baseball as the synonym for a deception or a dirty trick, and, as William Safire notes in *On Language:* "Because an old-time baseball pitcher never knew which way his spitball would break, the verb *to spitball* now means 'to speculate.' " The term's baseball origin probably goes back to 1902, when a pitcher named Frank Corridon accidentally discovered that a ball wet with saliva twisted and turned weirdly as it traveled to the plate. Corridon apparently told Chicago White Sox teammate Elmer Stricklett about his discovery and Stricklett perfected the pitch, even naming it when another teammate asked him what he called it: "Don't know. I suppose 'spitball' explains it as well as anything." Although other sources claim the *spitball* was invented by New Bedford pitcher Tom Dond in 1876, when he rubbed glycerine on the ball, the term is first recorded in 1904 and the Stricklett story seems more likely. Outlawed since 1920, the *spitball* was once a perfectly legal pitch in baseball. Many pitchers used it in its heyday and its unpredictable behavior made batters dread the pitch. Some modern-day pitchers have been charged with using the "spitter"—not usually by spitting on the ball anymore, but by more devious methods such as moistening the hands and scratching the ball. Schoolboy *spitballs* are even older than the baseball variety, as the word is first recorded in this sense in 1846. (*See* CURVEBALL.)

**SPOOF.** This word for a mocking imitation of something comes from the late-nineteenth-century board game called *spoof.* British comedian Arthur Roberts invented and named the then popular game, but no one has any idea where he got the name from.

**SPORT.** *Sport* is simply an abbreviation of the English word *disport,* "to amuse oneself," and is first recorded in about 1350. *Disport* itself is composed of the Latin *des,* "away," and *porto,* "carry"; *disport* originally meaning to carry away, especially to carry away from work, which is what one does by amusing oneself playing a *sport.*

**SPOT.** To *spot* someone something is to give him or her a handicap or concession. The expression is from billiards at a time in the early nineteenth century, when the standard game consisted of knocking a red ball into a pocket with the cue ball from a white spot on the table, leaving the cue ball in position to make another shot. Some players got so proficient that they could run twenty or more such *spot shots.* In order to equalize games with those less skillful, these experts granted their opponents a certain number of *spot shots* (as if they had made them). This became known as *spotting* an opponent points and added a new expression to the language.

**SQUEEZE PLAY.** The *squeeze play* or *squeeze play bunt* or *suicide squeeze* is said to have been invented by two Yale University players in 1897, but wasn't consciously used much or widely known until the 1905 major league season. It consists of a batter trying to "squeeze in" a run by laying down a bunt in a no-out or one-out situation when there is a runner on third base. The runner breaks toward home plate with the pitch and the batter tries to place the bunt in a spot from which the fielder can't throw the runner out at the plate. A *squeeze play* in American English also means to apply pressure on a person in order to gain an advantage or force compliance; this expression is possibly influenced by the baseball term. (*See* BUNT.)

**STACK THE DECK AGAINST.** *Stacking the deck against* someone is dishonestly prearranging something against that person. The expression has its origins in the age-old gambling practice of stacking a deck of cards, that is, prearranging them in order to cheat the other players.

**STALKING HORSE.** Hunters of old sometimes trained their horses to walk toward their quarry while the hunters remained hidden behind them until the game was within shooting range. Such horses were called *stalking horses* in the sixteenth century; it wasn't long before a *stalking horse* came to mean a sham political candidate used to conceal the candidacy of a more important figure in order to draw votes from a rival, or anything put forth to mask plans, any pretext.

**STAND ACE HIGH.** (*See* ACES.)

**STAND PAT.** American poker players in the late nineteenth century invented this expression to indicate that a player was satisfied with the original hand dealt and would draw no more cards. Where did the *pat* come from? One theory is that because the word meant "in a manner that fits or agrees with the purpose or occasion" or "incapable of being improved" it was a natural for the poker expression. Another holds that *stand pat* is a corruption of *stand pad,* an older English expression meaning "to sell from a stationary position" which originally referred to peddlers who remained in a fixed location. *To stand pad* was to remain fixed or firm, like a poker player who doesn't move to take any more cards. From poker, in any case, the expression passed into general use as a term for taking a firm, fixed position on something.

**STAND THE GAFF.** The *gaff* here is the sharp metal spur attached to the legs of cocks in cockfighting. A bird has to *stand* the slashes of such gaffs or lose the fight, which gave us the century-old expression *to stand the gaff,* meaning to weather hardship or strain, to endure patiently.

**STAR.** *Star,* for a sports figure of exceptional popularity or talent (or both), isn't some press agent's invention as many believe. The term was first used in baseball in 1880 but is over a century older and of theatrical origin. It is first recorded in a 1779 book on the theater in an appraisal of the great English actor David Garrick: "The little stars, who hid their diminished rays in his [Garrick's] presence, began to abuse him." *Star,* as a verb, wasn't used until about 1825. *Stardom* seems to have been coined by O. Henry in a 1911 short story.

**START FROM SCRATCH.** Unlike *to come up to scratch,* which probably derives from prizefighting, this was originally a horse racing expression. A *scratch* in England was the starting line in a horse race, and horses started there with no advantage besides their own ability, like anyone who *starts from scratch* in any undertaking. In this sense a *scratch race* is a race without restrictions as to the age, weight and winnings of the horses entered.

**START THE BALL ROLLING.** (*See* KEEP THE BALL ROLLING.)

**STAVE OFF.** A *stave* is a stick of wood, the word a back formation from the plural of staff, *staves.* In the early seventeenth century *staves* were used in the "sport" of bull-baiting, where dogs were set against bulls. Too often these contests were badly matched, for the bulls frequently had the tips of their horns removed, and when the dogs got a bull down, the bull's owner often tried to save him for another fight by driving the dogs off with a stave or stick. Because the owner actually "postponed" the bull's death until another day, the expression to *stave off* acquired its present figurative meaning of "to forestall." True or not, this is at least a possible explanation for *to stave off.*

**STEEPLECHASE.** According to one tradition, *steeplechase* originated with a race from church steeple to church steeple in Ireland's horse country. Another tale credits a group of British riders, returning home from a fox hunt, with inventing the sport and the word. These foxless riders decided to run a race in a direct line—regardless of obstacles—to the steeple of the village church; the winner would be the rider "who first touched the stones of the steeple with his whip." In any case, the original horseback races called *steeplechase races* had a church steeple in view as the goal and riders had to clear all the intervening obstacles. The word is first recorded in an 1805 issue of the British *Sporting Magazine.*

**STICK IT IN YOUR EAR.** This rude insult may have its origins in baseball, where *stick it in his ear* is often the cry of bench jockeys to a pitcher on their team who is facing a batter crowding the plate. Literally it means to hit the batter in the ear with the ball, but it usually means to throw the ball very close to the hitter, to dust him off. No one has determined exactly when this phrase came into the language but it was around in the 1950s. It may simply be a variation of ruder phrases like *stick it up your ass* and *shove it up your ass.*

**STICKLER.** The earliest *sticklers* were umpires or moderators at wrestling or fencing matches and tournaments in the sixteenth century. Within another hundred years the word was being used figuratively, followed by *for,* to describe anybody who unyieldingly insists on something, as in "He's a stickler for promptness." *Stickler* derives from the Anglo-Saxon *stihtan,* "to arrange or regulate."

**STICKY WICKET.** A *sticky wicket* is a difficult or awkward situation that calls for delicate handling, and this 1920s British expression still has some currency in the United States as a humorous term. It comes from the phrase *bat at a sticky* *wicket,* meaning to contend with great difficulties, which has its origins in cricket. In cricket a *sticky wicket* (goal) literally means that the area of ground around a wicket is soggy because of recent, heavy rain. This condition doesn't allow the ball to bounce well, making things difficult for the players trying to field it.

**STRAIGHT FROM THE HORSE'S MOUTH.** *Straight from the horse's mouth* means information or a tip that is supposed to be very reliable, from the source. This is probably a racetrack expression from the nineteenth century that, despite the uncertainty and unreliability of racing tips, became widely used off the track as well. However, another story holds that during the Peninsular Wars the offices of the secretary of war were in the old Horse Guards barracks in Whitehall, London. These old Horse Guard barracks were often the source of secret information—much to the duke of Wellington's displeasure—hence the expression *straight from the horse's mouth.*

**STRAIGHT FROM THE SHOULDER.** *Straight from the shoulder* means honestly, frankly, to the point, and derives from a boxing term of the mid–nineteenth century. A punch *straight from the shoulder* was once made by bringing the fist to the shoulder and sending it forward straight and fast. Such undeceptive blows are quick, effective and often to the point of the chin.

**STRIKEOUT.** In the American lexicon, *to strike out* means to fail completely; it is one of the most widely used baseball-derived terms. The baseball *strikeout,* a combination of three strikes, has been used in the sport since the 1840s. At first a *strike* meant just a missed swing at the ball or a fouled-off ball. There were no called strikes by the umpire until 1863; a strike is called when a ball is pitched within the strike zone (which is the area above home plate between the batter's knees and his armpits) and the batter doesn't take a swing at it. (*See* TWO STRIKES AGAINST YOU.)

**STYMIE.** To *stymie* something is to hinder, block or thwart it. The word derives from the golfing term *stymie,* first recorded in 1857, for a ball on a putting green lying between the cup or hole and the ball of an opponent. However, the golfing term itself may derive from the old obsolete Scottish expression *not to see a styme,* meaning not to see at all.

**SUDDEN DEATH.** *Sudden death* is sometimes used today to mean a fight to the finish (but not death) of any kind. It is mainly confined to football, where it indicates an overtime period in which a tied game is won by the team that scores first. There are *sudden death* periods in hockey and soccer too, but in basketball, the sport where the practice probably originated, overtime periods of a certain time duration are now played instead.

**SUGARED.** (*See* AIR BALL.)

**SULTAN OF SWAT.** Babe Ruth has carried this nickname since about 1920, when he joined the New York Yankees. Ruth was so named for his majestic swats of the ball, but the alliterative term was already in the language in reference to a real *sultan of Swat* (now part of Pakistan) who died in 1878 and inspired British poet Edward Lear to write:

> *"Who, or why, or which, or what*
> *Is the Akhoond [Sultan] of Swat"*

Lear's doggerel, in turn, may have inspired some sportswriter to name the Babe *the Sultan of Swat.* (*See* BABE RUTH.)

**SWEATERS.** The first garments called *sweaters* were heavy blankets fashioned to fit around a racehorse's body that trainers used in the early nineteenth century to induce profuse sweating during a workout on the track. The word is first recorded in this sense in 1828 and it was another thirty years before *sweater* was used to mean flannel underclothing that athletes wore when trying to work off weight. Finally, in 1882, the word *sweater* was applied to a woolen vest or jersey worn in rowing or other athletic activities, the direct ancestor of the *sweater* we know today.

**SWEEPSTAKES.** *Sweepstakes* is recorded as the name of a ship a century before the word *sweepstakes* was first used as a gambling term in 1593, but no one has been able to connect the ship with the gambling word in any way (or even explain the name of the ship!). *Sweepstakes* originally meant "winner take all," as if the winner *swept* all the *stakes* into his pocket after winning a game or race, although today multiple winners in sweepstakes have to divide the stakes between them.

**SWEETEN THE KITTY.** In the game of faro the "tiger" was the bank of the house, possibly because the tiger was once used on signs marking the entrance to Chinese gambling houses. Gamblers called the tiger a *kitty,* and it also became the name for the "pot" in poker and other card games. By the late nineteenth century *sweeten* or *fatten the kitty* had become a common expression for adding chips to the pot in a poker game, or for increasing the payment in any business deal.

**SWIM FINS.** Benjamin Franklin was America's first great swimmer and he even taught the sport in his early years. It was then that he invented and named *swim fins,* not the least of his myriad inventions considering the fun these flippers have brought to millions.

**SWITCH-HITTER.** There have been switch-hitters (hitters who can bat left-handed or right-handed) in professional baseball since at least 1870, when Robert V. Ferguson of the Brooklyn Atlanters batted this way. But the term *switch-hitter* may not have been coined until the 1920s. The word is now used generally to mean a versatile person and is also slang for a bisexual person.

# T

**TAKE IT ON THE CHIN.** To endure anything, especially pain, that fate deals out is the meaning of *to take it,* an American expression from boxing, where someone who *takes it* endures anything an opponent can dish out. The same thought is behind the expression *take it on the chin,* also from boxing. Both of the phrases now generally mean to take punishment or any adversity with courage and not let it defeat you.

**TAKE THE BULL BY THE HORNS.** Since the earliest quotation yet found for this expression is 1873, it seems unlikely that it has its roots in bull running, a brutal English sport that was popular from the day of King John until it was outlawed in the mid–nineteenth century. More likely the expression originated in Spain or America. In bullfights, Spanish *banderilleros* plant darts in the neck of the bull, then tire him by waving cloaks in his face and seizing him by the horns to hold his head down. Rawboned early ranchers in the American Southwest also wrestled bulls, or steers, in a popular sport called bull-dogging; still seen in rodeos, the object of this sport is to grab the animal's horns and throw him down. Either of these practices could have prompted the saying *take the bull by the horns* for "screw up your courage and cope with a dangerous or unpleasant situation decisively, head on."

**TAKE THE LONG COUNT.** A boxer knocked out *takes the long count,* that is he stays down at least until the referee counts

to ten. The American expression has also long been used in the past tense as a synonym or euphemism for death.

**TALK TURKEY.** According to an old story, in colonial days a white hunter unevenly divided the spoils of a day's hunt with his Indian companion. Of the four crows and four wild turkeys they had bagged, the hunter handed a crow to the Indian, took a turkey for himself, then handed a second crow to the Indian and put still another turkey in his own bag. All the while he kept saying, "You may take this crow and I will take this turkey," or something similar, but the Indian wasn't as gullible as he thought. When the spoils were divided, the Indian protested: "You talk all turkey for you. You never once talk turkey for me! Now I talk turkey to you." He then proceeded to take his fair share. Most scholars agree that it is from this probably apocryphal tale, first printed in 1830, that we get the expression *let's talk turkey,* "let's get down to real business."

**TALLYHO.** The cry *tallyho* originated on British fox hunts in the nineteenth century, where it was and still is, as far as I know, the cry of a hunter on first sighting the fox. The term is said to have its roots in the French hunter's cry of *tayau,* which dates back to about 1750. (*See* IN AT THE KILL.)

**TAROT.** *Tarot* is the French name of the popular central-European card game called *tarok,* which the *Encyclopedia Britannica* says is the world's oldest surviving card game. The game is named after Tar, the Egyptian god of the underworld, whom the Greeks called Tartarus. It has many features borrowed by other card games, including competitive bidding and the wild joker, and is now played with fifty-four cards, twenty-two of them trump card *tarots* bearing allegorical representations. These twenty-two illustrated cards, depicting vices, virtues and elemental forces, are the only ones used in the fortune-telling game called *tarot* that most people are familiar with.

**TATER.** *Tater* is baseball slang for a base hit or a home run. It possibly derives from the admiring expression *that's some potatoes* that fans early in the game's history would shout out after a player got a good hit.

**TAXI SQUAD.** In the late 1940s Art McBride, the original owner of the Cleveland Browns football team, had a number of players under contract to him who weren't on the active player list and could only play if one of his active players was injured and deactivated. Since this seemed like a waste of his money, he put these extra players to work as drivers in his taxi cab company. Soon all such players in the pro leagues were being called members of the *taxi squad*. Later, when the rules changed, the term was applied to the four extra players on a professional football team who aren't allowed to suit up for an official game but who are ready to join the team to replace injured or unsuccessful players.

**TEARING UP THE PEA PATCH.** Red Barber popularized this southern United States expression for "going on a rampage" when he broadcast Brooklyn Dodgers baseball games from 1945 to 1955, using it often to describe fights on the field between players. Barber hails from the South, where the expression is an old one, referring to the prized patch of black-eyed peas which stray animals sometimes ruined.

**TEE.** The first *tees* were just small handfuls of sand or dirt off which golf balls were hit. The Scottish word was first recorded in 1673 as *teaz*, but people thought this was the plural of *tee* and over the years *tee* became the singular form. The little wooden pegs we call *tees* today were invented by New Jersey dentist William Lowell in the 1920s.

**TEN, 10.** Ten, more often written as 10, means anything perfect—from a perfect woman or man to a perfect situation. The expression dates back to the early 1970s and may come from the sport of gymnastics, in which a ten is a perfect score on the scale of zero to ten.

**TENNIS, ANYONE?** *Tennis, anyone?* began life as *Who's for tennis?* in England about eighty years ago, also serving as a conversation opener or an ironic comment on the pastimes of the leisure classes. Eric Partridge believes it may have arisen "as a good-natured comment upon lawn tennis as an adjunct of tea parties in the vicarage garden or at countryhouse weekends," but it has also been suggested that the catch phrase comes from some turn-of-the-century English comedy of manners in which "an actor sprang through French windows calling, 'Anyone for tennis?' " (*See* LOVE.)

**TENNIS RACKET.** (*See* RACKET.)

**TEXAS LEAGUER.** A cheap hit that falls between the infield and the outfield in baseball is called a *Texas leaguer.* Back in 1886 three players who had been traded up to the majors from a Texas league enabled Toledo to beat Syracuse by repeatedly getting such hits. After the game, the disgusted Syracuse pitcher described the hits as just "little old dinky Texas leaguers," and the name stuck.

**TEXAS WEDGE.** A humorous golfing term not for a wedge or wedgie club but for a putter "when it can be used for a short approach shot over very flat, rather bare ground, as might be found in Texas," according to Stuart Berg Flexner in *Listening to America.*

**THAT RINGS THE BELL.** *That rings the bell* means that's perfect, just what we wanted. An Americanism first recorded in 1904, it almost certainly comes from the carnival game where a person tests his or her strength by driving a weight up a pole with a mallet. A contestant who rings the bell at the top of the pole wins the prize.

**THAT'S THE BALLGAME.** One would suspect that phrases like this, meaning that's the end of anything from a sports contest to an election, have been used since the first baseball game was played. So were expressions like *it's a whole new ballgame,* "it's a new beginning," and *it's the only ballgame in town,* "it's the only choice available."

**THAT'S THE WAY THE BALL BOUNCES.** This is the comparable sports phrase for "that's the way the cookie crumbles"—that's life, that's fate, that's the way it goes. Dating back to the 1950s, the phrase was apparently suggested by the way a ground ball can take a bad bounce just as a fielder is about to field it cleanly. This results in a hit instead of an out, or (in the outfield) an extra base hit instead of a single. It is a way of saying that despite every precaution one takes there are things beyond one's control; *C'est la vie.*

**THIMBLERIG.** *Thimblerig* is a slight-of-hand swindling game in which the operator palms a pea while appearing to cover it with one of three thimblelike cups, and offers to bet that no one can tell under which cup the pea lies. The name is first recorded in about 1815 and is still heard, but is mainly known as the *shell game* today after the walnut shells it is played with.

**THREEPEAT.** A brand new word, based on *repeat* and meaning to do something three times in a row, this expression seems to have been coined by New York Nicks coach Pat Riley in 1993, when the Chicago Bulls won the National Basketball Association title for the third straight year. Whether *threepeat* will last and pass into general usage remains to be seen.

**THROW.** When we say "Those tickets are a dollar a throw," we mean they are a dollar apiece. The expression possibly derives from those carnival games where players throw balls, hoops, rings, etc., trying to win a prize. *Throw* meaning to deliberately lose a fight or game is an American sports and gambling term from the mid–nineteenth century.

**THROW DOWN THE GAUNTLET.** The English language contains two wholly different words spelled and pronounced *gauntlet.* The *gauntlet* in this expression means glove and derives from the medieval French *gantelet,* "a little glove." Knights of the age of chivalry, though not so noble as they seem in romances, did play by certain rules. When one knight wanted to cross swords with another, he issued a challenge by throwing down his mailed glove, or gauntlet, and his challenge was accepted if the other knight picked up the metal-plated glove. This custom gave us the expression *to throw down the gauntlet,* "to make a serious challenge."

**THROWN FOR A LOSS.** Originally a football expression, *thrown for a loss* refers to the ball carrier who is thrown back for a loss by the opposing line on trying to penetrate its defense and gain yardage. Common in football, the words began to be used in the post–World War II years to describe someone's loss in any endeavor.

**THROW IN THE TOWEL.** *Throw in the towel* and *throw in the sponge*—both meaning to give up, quit or admit one has been defeated—have been around at least since the 1860s and probably date back to eighteenth-century England. The expression comes from boxing, where a fighter's manager throws a towel or sponge from the fighter's corner into the ring to stop the fight when he determines that his fighter has taken enough punishment and has no chance of winning. Figuratively, the colorful phrase came to mean the admission of defeat by anyone from a politician to a saint. Possibly the color of a white towel, suggesting a white flag of surrender, has helped the first variation endure.

**THROW SOMEONE A CURVE.** If you surprise someone in a negative way, deceive or mislead or ask a tricky question, you are *throwing someone a curve.* The expression has its roots in the curve of baseball, for a pitch that comes directly toward the batter and then breaks away, often surprising or tricking him. The first recorded mention of a *curveball* in baseball is 1874, but the pitch was introduced by Hall of Famer William Arthur "Candy" Cummings. (*See* CURVEBALL.)

**THUMBS DOWN.** First, we have the traditional story: *Habet!* or "He's had it," Roman spectators shouted when they wanted a defeated gladiator to be killed. Their shouts were accompanied by a kind of *thumbs-down* gesture that is believed to be the ancestor of the same gesture we use today and our expression *thumbs down* for "no!"

Some Latinists, however, say that *thumbs down* is a mistranslation of the Latin phrase *pollice verso,* which means "thumbs turned." According to this theory, spectators made the gesture *pollice primo,* "thumbs pressed," when a gladiator fought a good fight, and made the gesture *pollice verso* if he fought poorly and they wanted him killed. The idea that *pollice verso* meant "thumbs down," this story holds, seems to have been first suggested by a painting of nineteenth century French artist Jean Leon Gerome that depicted scowling Roman spectators holding their *thumbs down* at the end of a gladiatorial contest.

**THUNDERBOLT.** (*See* SHOOT ONE'S BOLT.)

**TINHORN GAMBLER.** In chuck-a-luck, an ancient dice game that was very popular during the gold rush, gamblers bet against the house that all three dice used would read the same when rolled; that the sum of all three dice would equal a certain number; or that one of the three dice would turn up a specified number. It is a monotonous game that was looked down upon by players of faro, a more complicated and costly pastime. Faro operators coined the name *tinhorn gamblers* for chuck-a-luck players, giving us this expression for any cheap gambler.

**TINKERS TO EVERS TO CHANCE.** This synonym for a routine double play in baseball should really be *Tinker to Evers to Chance,* referring as it does to the Chicago Cub infield combination of Joe Tinker (shortstop), Johnny Evers (second base) and Frank Chance (first base). All three are enshrined in baseball's Hall of Fame at Cooperstown, New York, but they aren't there for the double plays they executed. The vaunted trio only averaged fourteen twin killings a year from 1906–1909, the peak of their careers, which is very low for a double-play combo. Their fame is due principally to a famous Franklin P. Adams poem heralding them. It is said that Tinker and Evers were enemies who never spoke to each other off the field during their baseball careers.

**TOE THE LINE (OR MARK).** Before the Queensberry rules were devised, English prizefights were long and bloody. There was no footwork, and no tactics aside from dirty ones. No attempt was made to evade blows from an opponent. Their bare fists often hardened from soaking in walnut juice, fighters firmly placed their toes on a line officials marked in the center of the ring and slugged it out until one man fell, thus ending the round. The fighters then staggered or were dragged back to their corners for thirty seconds and the match continued until one man couldn't come out to *toe the line* when the bell rang for the next round. One of these bouts, the Burke-Byrne fight in 1833, lasted ninety-nine rounds, and poor Byrne—who never gave up—died from the beating he took. The sight of lurching, leaden-armed, broken-handed fighters *toeing the line* for hours at a time, and doing their job of battering each other bloody and senseless with superhuman willpower, inspired the saying *to toe the line,* "to do one's job, to live up to what is expected of you or conform with the rules." That the expression was an early one used in track events, meaning that all contestants must place their forward foot on the starting line ("Get ready, get on your mark . . .") also contributed to the popularity of this phrase.

**TOM THUMB GOLF.** *Tom Thumb golf* is a synonym for *miniature golf* (also known as *midget golf*), which is a game played with a putter and golf ball on a very short course that has many wooden and concrete obstacles. The game was invented around 1910. One of the first courses was built in Pinehurst, North Carolina, by landscape architect E. H. Wiswell and named "Thistle Dhu"—supposedly because Wiswell tired of the job and pronounced it finished, saying "This'll do."

**TOUCH ALL BASES.** Not touching a base in baseball can result in big trouble (*see* BONEHEAD PLAY) and even a player who hits a home run must touch all the bases as he rounds them, which led to the common general expression *to touch all bases,* to be thorough and leave nothing undone. This phrase, in turn, is the source of the expression *to touch base with,* meaning to consult or inform someone concerning an impending matter.

**TOWERING RAGE.** *Towering,* as used in several phrases, derives from a term in the sport of falconry. Castle watchtowers were the tallest structures in the Middle Ages, so high-flying hawks were said "to tower." *Towering ambition* is thus ambition that is beyond ordinary bounds, as high as the towering of a hawk. *Towering rage* or *passion* could both be explained in the same way—rage or passion mounting to its highest point—but there is an added dimension that strengthens the phrases. When a falcon "towers" she hovers at the height of her ascent searching for prey, ready to swoop down on her victim.

**TROPHY.** The ancient Greeks often marked places where they turned back the enemy in battle with monuments called *tropaions* (from the Greek *trope*, "putting to flight"). Such monuments—at first only such things as abandoned enemy equipment hung on a tree branch—later became battle monuments in public places and came to be called *trophies*. Eventually, *trophy* was used to describe any memento, such as a cup or a plaque, that is evidence of a victory or skill in sports.

**TRUDGEN STROKE.** John Arthur Trudgen (1852–1902), an outstanding British amateur swimmer, introduced the *Trudgen* or *Trudgen stroke* in 1893 after seeing it used in South America. The stroke, employing a double overarm motion and a scissors kick, is regarded as the first successful above-water arm action widely used in swimming. Trudgen popularized the idea of minimizing resistance by bringing the arms out of the water, which paved the way for the reception of the now common Australian crawl adopted from South Sea natives. The stroke was sometimes called the *Trudgeon,* a misspelling of the swimmer's name.

**TRUMP.** *Trump* or *trumps,* meaning a suit in card games outranking all other suits for the duration of a hand, is an old alteration of the word *triumph.* The word was first recorded in 1529 and apparently first meant both the name of a card game called *trump* and the term described above. Later the term spread to whist and then to bridge.

**TURN THE TABLES.** Collecting antique tables was a fad among wealthy men in ancient Rome, we're told. When these collectors chided their wives about expensive purchases, the women turned them toward these antique tables and reminded their husbands of their own extravagances, thus "turning the tables on them." A good story, but there is no evidence that it is true. The expression *to turn the tables* does not date from Roman times; it is only about four hundred years old, and may derive from the game of backgammon. In backgammon, formerly called "tables" in England, the board is usually divided into two "tables." One rule of the complicated game allows a player to double the stakes in certain situations and literally *turn the tables.* Another possibility is that the phrase comes from the old custom of reversing the table or board in chess, which enabled a player at a disadvantage to shift the disadvantage to his opponent. (*See* BACKGAMMON.)

**TWO DOWN, ONE TO GO.** When something is close to being accomplished, when the finish is near, one might say *two down, one to go.* The common expression is from baseball, where *down* is a synonym for "out" and has been used that way for over a century. There are of course three outs an inning allowed to a team at bat before the opposing team gets a chance to bat.

**TWO STRIKES AGAINST YOU.** When you have two strikes against you, you are close to striking out in baseball, a game in which a batter has three missed chances before his turn at bat is over. Thus we have the widely used phrase *to have two strikes against you*—borrowed from baseball, no one knows exactly when—meaning perilously close to losing, or, in another sense, starting out with an unfair disadvantage. (*See* STRIKEOUT.)

**TWO STRINGS TO ONE'S BOW.** This phrase means to be prepared for anything, to have an alternate plan. The expression is probably much older than its first recorded use, by Cardinal Wolsey in 1524, having its roots in the archer of ancient times who always carried at least two bowstrings when he went into battle.

# U

**UMPIRE.** *Umpire* is a later form of *noumpere,* which meant the same: "one who decides disputes between parties." *Noumpere,* in turn, ultimately derives from the Old French *nonper* (*non,* "not" plus *per,* "equal"). Thus, the idea behind the word is that the *umpire* is not equal to either party in a dispute, is the impartial third person. *Noumpere,* the accepted form up until the fifteenth century, began to be pronounced *umpire* because people transferred the *n* in the word to the indefinite article: *noumpere* becoming an *oumpere* and finally an *umpire.* In the same way a *napron* became an *apron,* a *nadder* became an *adder,* and an *ewt* became a *newt.* (*See* BLIND TOM; KILL THE UMP.)

**UNDER THE TABLE.** (*See* ABOVEBOARD.)

**UNDER THE WIRE.** (*See* JUST UNDER THE WIRE.)

**UPPERCUT.** An *uppercut* can be both a blow directed upward to an opponent's chin in boxing and a play in bridge of a higher trump than necessary. The boxing term, recorded in 1840, probably came first.

**UPPER HAND.** A nice story relates this expression to a fifteen-century gambling game almost identical to the way kids use a bat in choosing up sides for a sandlot baseball game. A stick was thrown to one man, who grabbed it, and the next man placed his hand just above the first man's. The game went on until the winner got the last, or upper, hand on the stick—the upper hand won, if he could throw the stick, which he often barely held by his fingertips, a distance previously agreed upon. The expression *upper hand,* however, is much older than the game, dating back to at least 1200. It derives from the earlier, obsolete *over hand,* which meant the same, the mastery or control "over" a person or thing.

**UPSHOT.** As far back as the early sixteenth century, an *upshot* meant the last shot in an archery contest, the shot that often determined the outcome of a match by forcing one archer to drop out and another to raise himself up in the standings. By the end of the century the now obsolete archery term had wider currency and came to mean any result or conclusion. Shakespeare, in fact, was one of the first to use the new word, in *Hamlet:* "So shall you hear . . . of accidental judgements . . . and in this upshot, purposes mistook."

**UP TO PAR.** (*See* PAR FOR THE COURSE.)

**USE HIM AS THOUGH YOU LOVE HIM.** It's not true that Izaak Walton said of the worm, as bait for fish: "Use him as though you loved him, that is harm him as little as you may possibly, that he may live the longer." He was referring to the frog when he wrote this in his classic *The Compleat Angler, or the Contemplative Man's Recreation* (1653), but his words became misinterpreted over the years, probably because fishermen use worms more than frogs.

**VARDON GRIP.** Harry Vardon (1870–1937), who won the British Open a record six times as well as the U.S. Open, is one of the outstanding golfers of all time. Born on the Channel Island of Jersey, Vardon also won eponymous fame for the *Vardon grip,* the overlapping grip used by most golf players today. The *Vardon trophy,* named in his honor, is awarded to the golfer with the lowest yearly average for the pro tour.

**VARSITY.** *Varsity,* for the first-string team of a United States college, high school or any school, is simply a shortened form of "university," the *varsity team* initially meaning the university team. In England, where the word is first recorded in 1846, *varsity* (formerly *versity*) means Oxford University or Cambridge University.

**VERONICA.** The classic Spanish bullfighting cape movement called the *veronica* takes its name from St. Veronica. In ancient legend she was the woman who wiped the face of Christ as he carried the cross, and her handkerchief retained an imprint of Christ's face. The cape movement is swung so slowly and near to the face of the bull that it suggested St. Veronica using her handkerchief.

**VIE.** In the sixteenth century, *envy* meant to challenge someone to a gambling contest. The word's contraction, *vie,* became popular in gambling houses, meaning to back up one's hand with a bet. One *vied* at cards in this way, that is, "contended or strived against others," and the term later came to mean contending or striving in any sense.

**VIGORISH.** Many people have paid usurious rates of interest to loan sharks. The margin of profit in such transactions, 20 percent or more per week plus late payment penalties and other fees, is called *vigorish,* which also means the percentage set by a bookmaker in his own favor. *Vigorish* is one of the few English words with Russian roots, deriving from the Russian *vyigrysh,* "gambling gains or profit," which first passed into Yiddish early in twentieth-century America as *vigorish* and was reinforced by its similarity to *vigor.*

**VOLLEYBALL.** When William Morgan, the YMCA director in Holyoke, Massachusetts, invented the game we call *volleyball* in 1895, he for some unknown reason called the new sport mintonette. Morgan, a Springfield College student himself, encouraged young people to play the sport and, as the volleying of the ball in it seemed the most exciting part of the game, its name was changed to *volleyball.* But a far better story anyway is playwright Arthur Kopit's apocryphal origin of the game, noted in Willard Espy's *Thou Improper, Thou Uncommon Noun* (1978): ". . . every evening in King Louis XV's prison compound a court official named Jacques de Vollet supervised eight nude chambermaids as they, four to a side, batted a loaf of sour bread hither and thither across a line draped with their underclothing. The bouncy play of the young ladies greatly agitated the manacled prisoners looking on. When the bread had been beaten into morsels too small to bat, the chambermaids tossed the remnants to the inmates for supper. Hence, logically, *volleyball.*"

# W

**WASHOUT.** Not all word derivations are cut and dried. Sometimes the same expression arises in two or more places from different sources, which may be the case with *washout,* both British and American slang for "a failure." British usage of this term derives from slang on the rifle range. After a team of riflemen had finished shooting at an iron target, the bullet marks in the bull's-eye were painted over with black paint and the rest of the target whitewashed to prepare it for practice by the next team. A shot completely off the target was called a *washout,* because it went off into the air and washed itself out, so to speak. This slang term for a missed shot, common in about 1850, became slang for a failure some fifty years later. However, before this, probably as early as the 1860s, *wash out* was an American term for the washing away by heavy rains of part of a road or railway. Some writers claim that this term independently suggested American usage of the expression *washout* for a failure, but there are no recorded instances of the figurative usage here until the 1920s. By that time, British and American forces had come in close contact during World War I. It seems likely that American soldiers borrowed the term for a failure from British slang without even realizing it, the *washout* of roads and railways being so familiar to them!

**WAVE A RED FLAG AT A BULL.** Though the bullfight matador waves his traditional red-lined cape to make the bull charge, it is the motion of the cape, not the color, that irritates the animal, as bulls are colorblind. Nevertheless, the image of the red cape long ago inspired the expression *to wave a red flag at a bull,* "meaning to do something that enrages someone."

**WELL-HEELED.** Before *well-heeled* meant "well provided with money" in American slang, it meant "well provided with weapons." Back in frontier days, men who went "heeled" carried a gun, the expression apparently deriving from a cockfighting term meaning "to provide a fighting cock with an artificial spur before he went into the pit." *Well-heeled* is recorded in this sense as early as 1867 and it wasn't until over a decade later that it took on the meaning it has today, perhaps because men found that it was easier and safer to protect themselves with money than with guns. In any case, *well-heeled* is not simply the opposite of *down at the heels,* someone so hard pressed for money that his shoes are run down at the heels.

**WELL, IF THAT DON'T TAKE THE RAG OFF THE BUSH.** This Americanism, an exclamation of surprise or wonder, dates back to the early 1800s. It may come from western shooting competitions where marksmen tried to shoot rags off bushes, or, since it also refers to outrageous behavior, might have originally referred to someone stealing rags (clothes) someone left spread out on a bush while in the swimmin' hole.

**WELLINGTON.** (*See* NAPOLEON.)

**WE WUZ ROBBED!** When Jack Sharkey won a decision over Max Schmeling in 1932 to take the world heavyweight championship, Schmeling's manager Joe Jacobs grabbed the radio fight announcer's mike and shouted, "We wuz robbed!" to a million Americans; his words are still a comic protest heard from losers in any endeavor. Jacobs's "I should of stood in bed'' is even more commonly used in fun. He said it after leaving his sickbed to watch the 1935 World Series in Detroit. According to John Lardner's *Strong Cigars and Lovely Women* (1951), *Bartlett's* is wrong in saying Jacobs made the remark to sportswriters in New York after returning from Detroit, and it had nothing to do with his losing a bet that Detroit would win the Series. Jacobs made the remark, Lardner says, in the press box during the opening game of the Series, when ''an icy wind was curdling his blood'' at the coldest ballgame anyone could remember.

**WHEEL.** I remember my father telling me to get my *wheel* out and we'd go for a ride. This synonym for a bicycle isn't heard much any more—at least I haven't heard it in years—but it is recorded as far back as 1880, probably suggested by the large front wheel of early bicycles, or, less likely, by unicycles, which date back twenty years or so earlier. There was, in fact, a bicycle manufacturer called the Chicopee Overman Wheel Company, which is also remembered in sports history for making the first basketballs at a time (about 1894) when soccer balls were being used in the infant game. (*See* BASKETBALL.)

**WHEELER-DEALER.** In gaming houses of the eighteenth-century American West, a big wheeler and dealer was a heavy bettor at cards and at the roulette wheels. Through this tradition, and the association of a *big wheel* as the man (or wheel) who makes the vehicle (things) run, the expression came to mean a ''big-time operator'' by the early 1940s. The term usually had an unsavory connotation, the *wheeler-dealer* being the type who runs over anything in his path with no regard for rules of the road.

**WHEN IN DOUBT, WIN THE TRICK.** (*See* ACCORDING TO HOYLE.)

**WHOLE SHOOTING MATCH.** Large crowds gathered at frontier shooting matches in America to watch marksmen compete in hitting targets, snuffing out candles, etc. *The whole shooting match* thus came to mean "the whole crowd in attendance" and, by extension, "the totality, everything, the whole thing." An earlier British phrase *the whole shoot*, meaning the same but with a different origin, may have strengthened the usage.

**WIDE OF THE MARK.** An ancient expression dating at least to the 1600s, this phrase means "inaccurate or erroneous, irrelevant." It probably comes from the sport of archery, referring to an archer's unsuccessful shot at the mark or target.

**WILD CARD.** The term *wild card* has been known in card games since the early sixteenth century, meaning "a card whose value is determined by the players in a particular game." Since then it has taken on special meanings in several sports, including tennis and football, and has come to mean generally anything outside of the normal rules or category, an unpredictable person, thing or event.

**WILD-GOOSE CHASE.** Englishmen in the late sixteenth century invented a kind of horse race called the *wild-goose chase* in which the lead horse could go off in any direction and the succeeding horses had to accurately follow the course of the leader at precise intervals, like wild geese following the leader in formation. At first the phrase *wild-goose chase* figuratively meant "an erratic course taken by one person and followed by another"; Shakespeare used it in this sense. But later the common term's origins were forgotten and a *wild-goose chase* came to mean "a pursuit of anything as unlikely to be caught as a wild goose"—any foolish, fruitless or hopeless quest.

**WIN HANDS DOWN.** A jockey who wins a race *hands down* is so far ahead of the field that he doesn't have to flick the reins to urge the horse forward and he crosses the finish line with his hands down, letting up on the reins. From racetrack slang toward the end of the last century, the metaphor *to win hands down* passed into general use for "any easy, effortless victory, a walkover."

**WINNING ISN'T EVERYTHING, IT'S THE ONLY THING.** The cynical remark is almost always attributed to Green Bay Packers coach Vince Lombardi in the 1960s. But it should be credited to a Hollywood script writer, having first been uttered by John Wayne, when playing a football coach in *Trouble Along the Way* (1953). (*See* IF JESUS WERE ALIVE TODAY . . .)

**WIN ONE FOR THE GIPPER.** This one is so well known, of course, because former President Ronald Reagan played George Gipp, or the Gipper, in a movie about Knute Rockne and his football team at Notre Dame (*Knute Rockne, All American,* 1940). Rockne urged his team to go out and "win this game for the Gipper," who on his deathbed had requested that the team win a game in his honor—and Notre Dame proceeded to do so. Actually, Gipp had made this request of Rockne in 1920 when dying of pneumonia and the coach had used the same appeal several other times before the 1928 game with the heavily favored Army team that is depicted in the film.

**WIN, PLACE AND SHOW.** The terms for the horses that finish first, second and third in a race, *win, place* and *show* originated at early United States racetracks where small boards were used to record the names of the first three finishers of every race. These boards were so small that only the names of the first two finishers were "placed" on the first board, *place* thus becoming the name for the number two horse. A second board was used to "show" the name of the third finisher and *show* became the common term for third place.

**WINTER GOLF.** Thousands of golfers don't let northern winters interfere with their outdoor golf games, braving the severest weather to play on the links. *Winter golf* is said to have been invented by British author Rudyard Kipling, a devoted golfer who painted his golf balls red so that he could play in the snow, but there were probably others who went to such extreme lengths before him.

**WITHIN AN ACE OF.** Dice, not cards, gave us this expression for "coming as close as one can get," the "ace" in the phrase referring to the ace, or small point, on a single die. Originally the expression was *within ambsace of,* "ambsace" being a mispronunciation of the Old French for the lowest possible throw in dice—*ambes as* ("both aces"). But by the seventeenth century, "ambsace" was further corrupted to "an ace" and the phrase became *within an ace of. Ambsace* itself was long a figurative term for bad luck. Today *snake eyes* is better known as the lowest throw in dice.

**WORK UP A SWEAT.** (*See* NOT TO TURN A HAIR.)

**WORLD-CLASS.** An athlete who competes in the Olympics or holds world records or approaches world records in a sport is said to be *world-class.* In recent times the term has been applied to people outstanding in anything, even negatively, as in "He's a world-class liar."

**WORLD SERIES.** This term is, of course, still used in baseball and has been extended to cover any highest-level contest, from the *world series* of poker to the *world series* of go-cart racing. The first World Series in baseball called the *World Series* was held in 1889, the term a shortening of the *World Championship Series.* This was a series of postseason games held each year between the pennant winners of the National League and American Association beginning in 1884. But the first World Series between two major league teams came in 1903, when the American League was recognized as a bona fide major league. The American League's Boston Pilgrims (later the Boston Red Sox) beat the National League's Pittsburgh Pirates in this best-of-nine game series, which fans paid one dollar a game to see.

**XANTHUS.** This is the name of Achilles's swift, magical horse in Greek mythology. Xanthus (pronounced *zăn-thŭs*) took his name from the Greek word for his reddish color. Among other magical feats, Xanthus could talk and predicted his master's death in battle. His name has been used through the centuries as the synonym for a great war horse or racer.

**"X" AS A SYMBOL.** The letter *X* is used as a English language symbol in many ways, including baseball scoring. When an unusual or extraordinary play occurs in a baseball game, the scorer marks it on his scorecard with an *X*.

**YACHT.** *Yachts* were originally pirate ships. The pleasure and racing craft takes its name from a type of speedy German pirate ship of the sixteenth century called the *jacht* that was common on the North Sea. A century later, British royalty found that this type of vessel made speedy pleasure boats and adapted the design, spelling the German word for them *yaught,* which finally became *yacht.*

**YANKEE.** The most popular of dozens of theories holds that the *Yankee* in the name of the New York Yankees comes from *Jan Kee,* "little John," a Dutch expression the English used to signify "John Cheese" and contemptuously applied to Dutch seamen in the New World and then to New England sailors. From a pejorative nickname for New England sailors, the term *Jan Kee,* corrupted to *Yankee,* was applied to all New Englanders and then to all Americans during the Revolution; the most notable example of this is found in the derisive song "Yankee Doodle." Nowadays, the British and others use *Yankee* for Americans, while southern Americans use it for northerners, and northerners use it for New Englanders, who are usually proud of the designation. *Yankee Clipper* was the nickname of New York Yankees star Joe DiMaggio, so called because his grace in the outfield reminded some sportswriter of a smooth-sailing clipper ship and/or because he consistently "clipped" the ball for hits.

**YARBOROUGH.** Little is known about Charles Anderson Worsley, the second earl of Yarborough, aside from the fact that he was a knowledgeable card player and made himself a small fortune, giving 1,000 to 1 odds that his bridge-playing companions held no cards higher than a nine. The odds were with the English lord, for the chances of drawing such a thirteen-card hand are actually 1,827 to 1 against. Yarborough, born in the early nineteenth century, died in 1897, an old and probably rich man. Since his wagers, a *Yarborough* has been any hand in whist or bridge with no card higher than a nine, although the term also means a hand in which there are no trumps.

**YOGIISM.** (*See* GOD SHOULD BE ALLOWED TO JUST WATCH THE GAME.)

**YOU CAN'T WIN 'EM ALL.** Baseball legend attributes the saying *you can't win 'em all* to Boston pitcher Clifton G. Curtis—who is a good choice, having lost twenty-three games in a row during the 1910–1911 seasons—but it probably goes back further. It is often used as a rueful expression said after one has failed at anything, or as a consoling remark to someone who has failed.

**YO-YO.** *Yo-yo,* the child's toy that spins up and down on a string, was once a trademark. This was true in 1929, when a Chicago toy maker patented the toy and was granted the trademark *Yo-Yo.* The manufacturer had noticed a Filipino youth playing with such a toy on the streets of San Francisco and purchased it from him. In his application for the trademark he claimed that he had coined the word *yo-yo* after noticing that children often shout "You! You!" to each other when playing some games. All he had done was to strike the *u* from these words, he explained. In any case, the novelty sold millions, and *yo-yo* contests were held throughout America, until a competitor marketed the same product under the same name. The Chicago manufacturer quickly brought suit for infringement of his trademark, but after hearing the evidence, the court ruled against him. It seems that his competitor offered incontrovertible evidence that he had been raised in the Philippines and as a boy had often played with a toy called a *yo-yo.* There was no doubt that the toy was of ancient Oriental origin and that it was long called by the Philippine name *yo-yo.* The court ruled that the trademark should never have been issued and today any manufacturer can use the term *yo-yo.* Today, a *yo-yo* is also a vacillating person, one whose opinions go back and forth like a *yo-yo;* it has also come to mean a stupid, obnoxious person.

# Z

**ZEBRA.** Referees in several sports, including football and basketball, wear black-and-white striped shirts while officiating games. Because of these colors, fans have been calling them *zebras* since about 1975.

**I ZIGGED WHEN I SHOULD HAVE ZAGGED.** This expression entered the language on April 17, 1939, when Jack Roper was knocked out in the first round of his fight with Joe Louis in Los Angeles. Roper, an unknown fighter in one of Louis's "bum of the month" bouts, had zigged and zagged, trying to dodge Louis's punches. When he came to, the fight's radio announcer asked him how he got tagged. *"I zigged when I should have zagged,"* he explained.

# Note on the Bibliography

Some of the best American writing over the past twenty-five years or so has been in the field of sports reporting and reminiscence. One has only to mention Roger Angell's *The Summer Game,* Jim Brosnan's *The Long Season* and Roger Kahn's *The Boys of Summer* to prove this point. A number of excellent sports reference works have also been published over this period, including Paul Dickson's *The Dickson Baseball Dictionary* and Joseph Reichler's *The Baseball Encyclopedia.* This bibliography of a hundred or so works includes many, if not all, of these relatively new books as well as American classics like Ring Lardner's *You Know Me, Al* and many more etymological reference works. Other books, articles and essays consulted are mentioned in the body of *Grand Slams, Hat Tricks and Alley-oops,* these ranging from popular poems like Ernest Thayer's immortal "Casey at the Bat" to the works of scholars here and abroad in learned magazines such as *Verbatim* and *American Speech.* Actually, a lifetime of reading has gone into this book and if I have neglected to mention a title, I offer my apologies for my lapse of memory.

# Bibliography

*American Heritage Dictionary of the English Language.* New York: American Heritage Publishing Co., Inc., 1969 and 1992 editions.

Angell, Roger. *The Summer Game.* New York: Popular Library, 1972.

Asimov, Isaac. *Words From the Myths.* Boston: Houghton Mifflin, 1961.

Asinof, Eliot. *Eight Men Out.* New York: Henry Holt, 1987.

Barber, Red, and Robert Creamer. *Rhubarb in the Catbird Seat.* New York: Doubleday, 1968.

Bartlett, John R. *Dictionary of Americanisms.* Boston: Little, Brown & Company, 1848, 1859, 1877.

Berrey, Lester V., and Melvin Van Den Bark. *The American Thesaurus of Slang.* New York: Thomas Y. Crowell Company, 1962.

Bloomfield, Leonard. *Language.* New York: Henry Holt & Co., 1933.

Blumberg, Dorothy Rose. *Whose What?* New York: Holt, Rinehart & Winston, 1969.

Bodmer, Frederick. *The Loom of Language.* New York: W. W. Norton & Company, 1944.

Bombaugh, C. C. *Oddities and Curiosities of Words and Language.* Edited by Martin Gardner. New York: Dover Publications, 1961.

Bouton, Jim. *Ball Four.* Cleveland: World, 1970.

Brewer, E. Cobham. *A Dictionary of Phrase and Fable.* New York: Harper & Row, 1964.

Bridgewater, William, and Elizabeth J. Sherwood. *The Columbia Encyclopedia.* New York: Columbia University Press, 1950.

Brosnan, Jim. *The Long Season.* New York: Dell, 1961.

Brown, Ivor. *A Word in Your Ear.* New York: E. P. Dutton & Co., 1963.
———. *I Give You My Word.* New York: E. P. Dutton & Co., 1964.
———. *Just Another Word.* New York: E. P. Dutton & Co., 1963.
———. *Say the Word.* New York: E. P. Dutton & Co., 1964.
———. *Words in Our Time.* London: Jonathan Cape, 1958.
Bulfinch, Thomas. *Bulfinch's Mythology* (1855). New York: Random House, 1993.
Chapman, Robert, ed. *New Dictionary of American Slang.* New York: Harper & Row, 1986.
Ciardi, John. *A Browser's Dictionary.* New York: Harper & Row, 1980.
———. *Good Words to You.* New York: Harper & Row, 1987.
Claiborne, Robert. *Loose Cannons and Red Herrings.* New York: Ballantine Books, 1989.
Coffin, Tristram. *The Old Ballgame.* New York: Herder, 1971.
Considine, Tim. *The Language of Sport.* New York: Facts on File, 1982.
Dickson, Paul. *The Dickson Baseball Dictionary.* New York: Avon Books, 1991.
*Dictionary of American Biography.* 20 vols. New York: Charles Scribner's Sons, 1928–37, supplement 1, 1944; supplement 2, 1958.
*Dictionary of American Regional English,* Frederick C. Cassidy, Chief Editor, volumes 1 & 2. Cambridge, Mass.: Belknap Press, 1985 & 1991.
*Encyclopedia Britannica,* 1957 edition.
Ernst, Margaret S. *More About Words.* New York: Alfred A. Knopf, 1964.
Evans, Bergen. *Comfortable Words.* New York: Random House, 1962.
Farmer, John S., and W. E. Henley. *Slang and Its Analogues.* 7 vols. New Hyde Park, N. Y.: University Press, 1966.
Flexner, Stuart Berg. *I Hear America Talking.* New York: Van Nostrand, 1976.
———. *Listening to America.* New York: Simon & Schuster, 1982.
Frommer, Harvey. *Sports Roots.* New York: Atheneum, 1979.
———. *Sports Lingo.* New York: Atheneum, 1979.
Funk, Charles Earle. *A Hog on Ice.* New York: HarperCollins, 1985.
———. *Heavens to Betsy! and Other Curious Sayings.* New York: HarperCollins, 1986.
———. *Thereby Hangs a Tale.* New York: HarperCollins, 1985.

———, and Charles Earle Funk, Jr. *Horsefeathers and Other Curious Words.* New York: HarperCollins, 1986.

Funk, Wilfred. *Word Origins and Their Romantic Stories.* New York: Funk & Wagnalls, 1950.

Garagiola, Joe. *Baseball Is a Funny Game.* New York: Bantam, 1962.

Garrison, Webb. *What's in a Word?* New York: Abingdon Press, 1965.

———. *Why You Say It.* New York: Abingdon Press, 1955.

Goldberg, Isaac. *The Wonder of Words.* New York: Frederick Ungar Publishing Co., 1957.

Grose, Francis. *A Classical Dictionary of the Vulgar Tongue.* Edited by Eric Partridge. London: Routledge and Kegan, Paul, 1963.

Hargrove, Basil. *Origins and Meanings of Popular Phrases and Names.* Philadelphia: J. B. Lippincott Co., 1925.

Hart, James D., ed. *The Oxford Companion to American Literature.* New York: Oxford University Press, 1956.

Harvey, Sir Paul. *The Oxford Companion to Classical Literature.* Oxford: Clarendon Press, 1955.

———, ed., *The Oxford Companion to English Literature.* Oxford: Clarendon Press, 1955.

Hayakawa, S. I. *Language in Thought and Action.* New York: Harcourt Brace Jovanovich, 1949.

Hollander, Zander. *Baseball Lingo.* New York: Norton, 1968.

Holt, Alfred H. *Phrase and Word Origins.* New York: Dover Publications, 1961.

Hunt, Cecil. *Word Origins, The Romance of Language.* New York: Philosophical Library, 1949.

Jennings, Gary. *Personalities of Language.* New York: Thomas Y. Crowell Company, 1965.

Kahn, Roger. *The Boys of Summer.* New York: Harper & Row, 1972.

Lardner, Ring. *You Know Me, Al.* University of Illinois Press, 1992.

Mathews, Mitford M., ed. *Dictionary of Americanisms.* Chicago: University of Chicago Press, 1951.

McFarlan, Donald, ed. *Guinness Book of Records.* New York: Bantam Books, 1992.

Mencken, H. L. *The American Language.* 3 vols. New York: Alfred A. Knopf, 1936–48.

Menke, Frank G., ed. *New Encyclopedia of Sports.* New York: A. S. Barnes & Co., 1963.

Morris, William, and Mary Morris. *Dictionary of Word and Phrase Origins.* 3 vols. New York: Harper & Row, 1962.

Onions, C. T. *The Oxford Dictionary of English Etymology*. London: Oxford University Press, 1966.

*Oxford Dictionary of Quotations*. London: Oxford University Press, 1954.

*Oxford English Dictionary and Supplements*. Oxford: Clarendon Press, 1990.

Partridge, Eric. *A Dictionary of Catch Phrases*. Stein & Day, 1977.

———. *A Dictionary of Slang and Unconventional English*. New York: Macmillan, 1985.

———. *Dictionary of Clichés*. New York: Routledge, 1978.

———. *From Sanskrit to Brazil*. London: Hamish Hamilton, 1952.

———. *Origins*. London: Routledge and Kegan Paul, 1958.

Pei, Mario. *All About Language*. Philadelphia: J. B. Lippincott Co., 1954.

Peterson, Harold. *The Man Who Invented Baseball*. New York: Scribners, 1973.

Pyles, Thomas. *Words and Ways of American English*. New York: Random House, 1952.

Radford, Edwin, and M.A.M. Radford, eds. *Encyclopedia of Superstitions*. New York: Philosophical Library, 1945.

———. *Unusual Words and How They Came About*. New York: Philosophical Library, 1946.

*Random House Dictionary of the English Language*. New York: Random House, 1987.

Reichler, Joseph, ed. *The Baseball Encyclopedia*. New York: Macmillan, 1985.

Rice, Grantland. *The Tumult and the Shouting*. New York: A. S. Barnes, 1954.

Safire, William. *What's the Good Word*. New York: Avon, 1983.

———. *I Stand Corrected*. New York: Times Books, 1984.

Shipley, Joseph T. *Dictionary of Word Origins*. New York: Littlefield, Adams & Company, 1967.

Skeat, Walter W. *An Etymological Dictionary of the English Language* (rev. ed.). London: Oxford University Press, 1963.

Sperling, Susan Kelz. *Tenderfoot and Ladyfingers*. New York: Viking Press, 1981.

Stevenson, Burton, ed. *Home Book of Quotations* (revised). New York: Dodd, Mead & Co., 1947.

———. *The Home Book of Proverbs, Maxims, and Familiar Phrases*. New York: Macmillan, 1948.

Taylor, Isaac. *Words and Places*. London: Dent, 1911.

*The Random House Dictionary of the English Language.* New York: Random House, 1966.

Urdang, Laurence. *A Fine Kettle of Fish.* Detroit: Visible Ink Press, 1991.

*Webster's New Twentieth Century Dictionary,* Unabridged. 2d ed. New York: World Publishing Company, 1966.

*Webster's Word Histories.* New York: Merriam-Webster, 1989.

Weekley, Ernest. *Concise Etymological Dictionary of Modern English.* New York: E. P. Dutton & Co., 1924.

———. *The Romance of Words.* New York: Dover Publications, 1961.

Wentworth, Harold and Stuart Berg Flexner. *Dictionary of American Slang.* New York: Thomas Y. Crowell Company, 1960.

# Index

# INDEX

# Index